MARRIAGE MATTERS!

D0106605

Shaw Books by Stuart Briscoe

Foundations of the Faith Series

The Apostles' Creed: Beliefs That Matter

The Fruit of the Spirit: Cultivating Christian Character

The Ten Commandments: Playing by the Rules

Understanding the Book Series

1 Peter: Holy Living in a Hostile World

Philippians: Happiness Beyond Our Happenings

Books by Jill Briscoe

Heartbeat

Renewal on the Run: Encouragement for Wives
Who Are Partners in Ministry

Books by Stuart and Jill Briscoe

Living Love: What Can Happen When We
Learn to Love God's Way

Stuart & Jill Briscoe

Marriage MATTERS!

Growing through the differences and surprises of life together

Harold Shaw Publishers
Wheaton, Illinois

Library of Congress Cataloging-in-Publication Data

Briscoe, D. Stuart.
  [Pulling together when you're pulled apart]
  Marriage matters! : growing together through the differences and surprises of life together / Stuart and Jill Briscoe.
    p. cm.
  Originally published: Pulling together when you're pulled apart.
Wheaton, Ill. : Victor Books, c1991.
  ISBN 0-87788-532-X
  1. Marriage—Religious aspects—Christianity. 2. Clergy—Family relationships. 3. Family—Religious life. 4. Briscoe, D. Stuart. 5. Briscoe, Jill. I. Briscoe, Jill. II. Title.
BV835.B724 1994
248.8'44—dc20   93-405832
                                           CIP

99 98 97 96 95 94

10 9 8 7 6 5 4 3 2

CONTENTS

To our children and their partners:

Dave and his Debbie,
Judy and her Greg,
Pete and his Libby

*We trust their love stories will also be
an open book that will benefit their
own generation for Christ.*

PREFACE

People are everywhere in our lives—shouting for our attention, looking to us to meet their expectations and their needs. Then there are the opportunities and demands of ministry—good things that "must" be done and others that "could" be done, if we just stretch and reach a little bit more.

It's often difficult for us to know how much is too much! "Who is the most important? Which bit of me do I give to whom?" you may ask. And then you may wonder, *After I've given my energy to my spouse, my children, my friends, my church, what's left for me?*

We know how you feel. That's why we wrote this book. We hope it gives you a little bit of encouragement to know that God is for you, and for your marriage and family. God believes that marriage matters—tremendously! We trust this book will help you in your own marriage as you travel through ours, growing through the surprises, celebrating the differences.

Stuart and Jill

There's No Place Like Home

Stuart

I must have dozed off. But the familiar jolt and *thump* of landing gear and roaring reverse-thrust engines brought me back to awareness. And what an awareness! Low-grade headache, buzzing ears, lower back locked in an uncomfortable place, eyes gritty with sleeplessness, enough stomach acid to burn a hole in concrete, and legs that felt as if they belonged to someone else. Jet lag for the thousandth time! But I was home again.

Thirty hours earlier I'd boarded a 747 in Johannesburg, South Africa, and here I was in Milwaukee, Heartland U.S.A. Spending that amount of time on airplanes is not the best way to live a life, but it beats the way they used to do it! Oxcarts and Mayflowers and wild Indians and that kind of thing. They didn't get jet lag, but they didn't get around as much either.

It was only two weeks since I'd left home, but I'd been in Omaha, Minneapolis, London, Cape Town, Johannesburg, Boston, and Detroit—and that's getting around. I'd said good-bye to Jill early on a Monday morning. We'd held each other, prayed for each other, and reluctantly parted, and as

I climbed into the car she'd said quietly, with soft eyes, "I love you, and I'll miss you, and I'll be praying."

"Same here, honey," I'd replied, driving off and catching sight of her in the rearview mirror, standing there with her thoughts. Thirty-one years of marriage to her, full of good-byes, had not made parting easier as we had thought it would. But thirty-one years of "welcome home" had gotten better and better, as we had hoped it would.

I'd explained to her, as I left, that I had a typical Monday full of staff meetings, desk work, worship service planning sessions, counseling, TV shows to tape, and then the monthly elders' meeting that could easily stretch into Tuesday. So I'd planned to go straight to the airport, check into a hotel in the early hours, and catch the first flight to Omaha.

"Is Omaha on the way to South Africa?" she'd asked.

"Depends where you start out," I replied.

A typical conversation between us! Despite the fact that she had traveled the globe, she still had only a nodding acquaintance with geography. Her capabilities for getting lost were legendary, and my tendencies to tease her for it were equally well known. But she didn't mind—in fact, she welcomed it because she'd often said to me that the surest sign that I was irritated or upset was that I stopped teasing her!

As I waited for my bags to arrive on the carousel I phoned her. The low, gentle hello at the other end was warm, predictable, welcoming, and comfortably familiar. The gentle voice of Jill—the voice of home. I'd called her from Johannesburg using a portable phone, standing under flowering jacaranda, incredibly beautiful in the lavender blossom—a world away. Now I was a forty-five-minute drive away from a hug, kisses, a typical English cup of tea, and an excited recital by her of everything that had happened while I was away.

In the early days I used to be somewhat put out that she was so full of what she'd been doing that she didn't give me a chance to say what I'd been doing! One day I interrupted her and said, "I had a great time too!" She was embarrassed by her thoughtlessness; I was embarrassed by my pettiness—but we have long since made the adjustments necessary in a marriage of two people better known for talking than listening. We have learned to take turns talking and listening. In fact, at one stage we even considered using an egg timer!

Getting home again this time would be extra special. The day before I'd left home I'd been preaching about the church in Antioch and, among other things, had pointed out the importance of the prophetic ministry in the experience of that church. Without going into too much detail here, I had encouraged the congregation to consider the various understandings of *prophecy* in the contemporary church and had left open the possibility that God could communicate to us in this way today. On the way to Omaha I'd called Jill from Minneapolis to tell her about the elders' meeting, but I didn't get the chance. There was a worried tone in her voice as she'd answered the phone.

"Stu, I just got a call from someone in the congregation who said that he had awakened in the middle of the night with a strange feeling that you should not leave the country. He was very sensible about it, said he'd never experienced anything like it before, and hoped we wouldn't feel he was weird in telling us what he felt." Then she added, "I can't explain it either, but I woke up this morning with a heavy sense of dread. It was nameless and unidentifiable but real. I couldn't sleep so I spent time in prayer and reading and came across the verse about dread: 'There they were, overwhelmed with dread, where there was nothing to dread' (Psalm 53:5). Our special prayer circle is here for breakfast and prayer this morning. We feel we should all wait on the Lord, but right now we see no clear reason for you not to go."

At that moment my flight for Omaha had been called, but Jill added, "Don't forget I'm going to California this afternoon."

"I'll call you tonight," I promised. But I never did because I couldn't contact her.

As she was flying west, the captain of her flight had announced, "We've just heard that there has been a major earthquake in the Bay Area. We think we can land in Los Angeles, although air traffic has been severely disrupted." Later, as they had approached their destination, he had made the remarkable announcement, "Folks, there are so many planes stacked up out there that I suggest you draw your blinds!"

Jill at one time had been very frightened of flying—I suppose you could say paranoid—but she had experienced a great measure of freedom from fear through prayer and trust in the Lord. However, this time the butterflies had flown by in formation in the pit of her stomach as they landed at the crowded airport.

I had been busy in Omaha, teaching a seminar for Salvation Army officers, while all this was going on. When I heard about the earthquake and remembered my promise to call her in Los Angeles, I tried, but communications were chaotic. It seemed everybody wanted to call California. Eventually I got through to her hotel and talked to a Mrs. Briscoe, only to find there were two of them in the hotel and I'd gotten the wrong one! It turned out that Jill's phone was out of order and they had never fixed it.

As I'd made the decision to fly to South Africa as planned, I called my secretary to contact Jill as soon as possible and tell her I would call from London. I wondered how many other people had marriages like ours. There had always been tension between marriage expectations and ministry obligations. We were no strangers to decisions, big decisions having to be made based on prayer and spiritual promptings. Not infrequently we had known the sharp edge of criticism from those who did not always agree with the way we had interpreted and experienced the uniqueness of our marriage.

But now I was finally home. As we sipped our obligatory cups of tea, the stories of the previous two weeks spilled out: Jill's experience of a deep sense of peace and confidence despite the uncertainties and trauma of what she had gone through; my testimony to a clear sense of commitment to going to South Africa, although I admitted to some degree of concern. Why the message not to leave the country? We had a pregnant daughter and a pregnant daughter-in-law (with twins). Were they going to need me? Was Jill going to be all right in California if San Andreas faulted again? Was the turmoil always slightly below the South African surface going to break out in violence? Or ought I to finish the tests on my heart that we had started to see why I was experiencing tightness in my chest? But here we were together again, I in my small corner and Jill in hers.

There's nothing like a cup of tea from your own mug that states, humbly, "World's Greatest Granddad," back in your old sweatsuit, in your own chair, listening to your own wife tell about the week's ministry at Biola University, and when she takes a breath, telling her about remarkable response to ministry at St. James Church in Cape Town and Randburgh Baptist Church in Johannesburg. And when I pause, to hear about Judy and Greg's prenatal class, Dave and Debbie's sonogram, which shows twin boys (and they already have two!), and Pete and Libby's move to Illinois to be nearer Trinity Divinity School, where Pete is studying. The phone calls, the mail, and the staff questions can wait till morning. Now it's sleepy time. My own bed, my own wife, my own marriage, my own . . . sleep. Bliss.

Love at Second Glance

Jill

$\mathscr{K}$neeling by my pretty little white bed in my bedroom in Liverpool, England, I made a wish list that had to do with the man of my dreams. Before I had become a committed Christian I would have compiled a very different list of wishes on that paper. I would have ordered a man of means that could show me a good time, be inordinately handsome, athletic, keep me in the lap of luxury, send our kids to the best English schools—and of course love and pamper me to death!

Now my pen hesitated as it hovered over the paper. Yes, I would want a man to love me deeply and to have the ability to provide for us. Above all I would want him to provide for the happy little family we would have together. But *what* to provide was now in question. My dreams and whole focus had changed.

I had become a Christian! I had truly believed I was one already. Therefore, it had been a complete shock to learn I needed to do more than tip my intellectual hat in the direction of heaven at Easter and Christmastime. Having lived for eighteen happy, eventful, but certainly self-centered years without the apparent necessity to rely on God—except for exams, visits to the dentist, and when I got into the finals of tennis tournaments—someone explained

1

the whole thing to me during a stay in the hospital. Of course it made absolute sense. It was obviously true. And so I became what I had thought I was—a real Christian—as opposed to a pretend one. Immediately I noticed profound changes in my thought patterns, behavior, and aspirations. Even my ideas on marriage were different than they had been. Now I wanted only a man who would love God first (though I didn't fully comprehend what that really meant) and would insist on serving him. It certainly would be nice if he could be good-looking and athletic too, but that was not essential anymore. I wasn't even sure about the pampering-me-to-death bit.

I played with my list, finished it, and then knelt down by my bedside. I very shyly showed it to a God I couldn't see, a Christ I had only just come to trust, and a Holy Spirit I could hardly comprehend. I sort of introduced the man of my dreams to the Trinity, to the Dream Makers, and asked if it were possible they could dream up someone to match my list.

As I knelt there on that sleepy English summer evening, I heard a little voice. It wasn't a human voice or a weird sound in my head; it was an insistent, demanding, still small voice in my spirit that wouldn't be quiet. I knew at once who was speaking and what he was saying.

"Jill, give me your list!"

"Why, Lord?" I asked somewhat apprehensively. "Can't you read it from there?"

"Oh, yes," the little voice answered, smiling. (I didn't know a voice could smile, but I knew this One could and was.) "You know perfectly well I can see it, but I don't want to read it. I want to keep it."

I knew then that I had come to a very important moment in my life. If I let go of my precious wish list, my dreams might never be fulfilled. I wouldn't be in control anymore. God would be the one who would decide if a man fit into the Big Plan (The Big Plan being his plan for my life) or not.

I didn't like losing control of anything. But as I thought about it, I realized it wasn't a question of losing control but of giving control. I also knew a pair of heavenly hands were not going to reach through my little pink and white bedroom ceiling and snatch my list away from me. No, it was up to me. At that moment I had a choice to make. I had to choose who was going to choose.

How long I knelt there I can't remember. A long, long time. In the end I held up my list and let it fall onto the bed, imagining it landing in a beautiful pair of tanned, strong, rugged, nail-pierced hands. After all, I thought, he gave up his list for me. He never married. He let his Father choose for him. There were a few tears—I wondered if I would ever have a husband. But giving him the list gave me a vivid picture to remember. Now every time a neat Christian man came into sight I would see that piece of paper with all my hopes and dreams written all over it fluttering down into his hands, and I would remind myself I didn't have a vote. It was up to him. It didn't mean I would marry, and it didn't mean I wouldn't. It meant that the decision would be made in a higher court.

About eight months later I was invited to supper by a young Christian couple who had become my friends and had taken me under their wing. They encouraged me to take the wild group of kids I had been working with to a Christian youth center called Capernwray Hall, in the beautiful English lake district. Returning from college, I had become involved with a group of my peers who wanted to share their Christian faith with others who didn't believe. This had led us to invest our free time in going where the kids were (definitely not in church!) and trying to interest them in the Christian faith. A few of these typical youngsters who hung around the fish-and-chip shops, coffee bars, and parks showed some interest. So we hired a room, invited them in, and began to argue through the basics of Christian doctrine.

Contrary to their belief, we assured them God was not dead even though mankind had done their best to make sure he was finished off. He rose again despite the worst we could do to him, and he lives today. He had died for us to save us by bearing the awesome consequences of our sin. Christianity was not just something to believe but had to do with Someone to relate to. We tried to explain an indwelling Christ who could make Christian behavior possible. This was quite logical, we argued. Christ was the only one in the whole world who had lived a perfect Christian life, so it followed he could do that again in our lives—in our bodies if we asked him to.

Never having been to church, the kids were hearing these things for the very first time. Some believed, invited Christ by his Spirit to come into their lives, and began to live out their belief. The inevitable result was radically changed teens. The problem was that these teenagers worked in an unbelievably hostile environment in which they found themselves constantly swimming against the stream. The suggestion that we take them out of their environment to a Christian camp sounded like a great idea. Getting these new Christians into an encouraging atmosphere where their faith could have room to breathe and a chance to grow and flourish was obviously the way to go. Anyway, I thought I'd learn what to do with them next, seeing that I was a total novice in such matters. Taking the youth center brochure from my friends, I looked at the front of it. Little did I dream that the gorgeous English manor house on the cover would later become my home!

The talk over supper that evening ranged from the needs of the teenagers to really know Christ, to our faith and fears, our hopes and our dreams. I hesitantly shared my struggles to be a "happy" single. "I know the Lord says singleness is a gift," I confided, "but I'm tempted to tell the Giver I'd rather he offered me the gift of marriage!" I wondered aloud if I would ever find the man of my dreams, and I told them about my intimate struggle with my wish list.

"Maybe God knows you would serve him best with that longing satisfied," my friends said. But they also encouraged me to unwrap the gift of singleness and enjoy it for a while, till we saw what God would decide. And so I tried to do that.

It was Easter in the lake district when we arrived at Capernwray Hall. Daffodil and bluebell time, rhododendron and snowdrop time. The tender season "when a young man's fancy lightly turns to love" (and a young woman's fancy too, I was soon to discover!). Only having been Christians for a brief period, the teens and I were overwhelmed with the atmosphere that pervaded that place. The countryside was a far cry from the concrete parks in Liverpool and took not a little getting used to. Stiletto heels and mini-skirts weren't the best gear for tramping through the fields, and there were no fish-and-chip shops around, although the noisy, happy coffee shop was soon packed out with appreciative customers.

"Where's Woolworth's?" a tall, tough boy asked, gazing at the hills and dales with no visible joy.

"No Woolworth's for a week," I told him. "You'll survive; you'll see!" And he did. There were so many believers there, all enjoying clean fun and terrific recreation, exhibiting an evident relish of life. There were great speakers in the lively meetings who broke big truths small enough for all of us to digest, yet made us stretch and reach for a breadth of spiritual understanding that shook us to our socks.

"I hope my soul has elastic sides or it will burst with all this stuff," a teenager said with a grin, wide-eyed and wondering. "And this music isn't like singin' 'ims" (she meant hymns). The leaders were skilled in using contemporary Christian music and putting into words things that should be happening in our lives if we wanted to grow as Christians. All of us were eager to be shown the way.

"Christ is living in you, and it's his business to win souls," one speaker explained.

"Of course!" we excitedly responded. Hadn't he been influencing our friends as we struggled to articulate our newfound spiritual experience? However awkwardly, we had lent our eager lips to God to explain our awakened hearts, enlightened minds, and regenerate souls to others. Somehow a power had been working right along with us, in us, and through us convincing our friends of the truth of it all. Now we understood the risen Christ by his Spirit was living in us to do these very things. The Bible said so! The talks were never too long, the interaction never less than challenging; the very air we breathed seemed to be incredibly alive around us. If the excited noise of two hundred teenagers would have ever subsided, I thought we would surely have heard the sound of angels' wings! We reveled in it all. We agreed we all felt we had come in out of the cold. We had arrived "home" after living among strangers.

One day I glanced around the long communal lunch table and couldn't help but notice a tall, extremely attractive fellow thoroughly enjoying himself. I glanced his way a second time and found him glancing at me. He and four or five other friends seemed to be the focal point of interest. They told the funniest jokes, and the loudest and wildest things seemed to happen when they were around. The fun, the joy, and the exuberance of their lively style took my breath away. One day I played a table tennis match with a girl who was talking to this particular young man. He came along to watch, and afterwards we played doubles.

After the game I took a long walk in the rolling English countryside and reminded my heart that I was working on being a happy single. But I noticed my heart wasn't listening! Two days later the young man in question was introduced to me as he was leaving the conference. (Being very English, we needed a proper introduction!)

"I'm Stuart Briscoe, and I work on the inspection staff of a bank," he told me. He would shortly be coming to my hometown on business, he said. I shared some of my concerns with him about the young people I had brought with me. "I do quite a lot of work with teenagers myself," he replied. "Maybe I could help." He took my address, and then he was gone.

By now my heart wouldn't stop smiling, and I began to worry about the plans that God and I had made. "Don't let me get sidetracked, Lord," I prayed. "I really want to go to Bible school and maybe to Africa for you." However could being a banker's wife fit into that idea, I wondered.

A week later, our group, by now charged up and ready to win the world, was back home and into the swing of things again. As I prepared a school lesson in my room, the doorbell rang. A deep, cheerful, unusually distinctive voice asked for me! "Lord, what are you doing to me?" I demanded. My heart was leaping up and down as it hadn't done since my very first romance at the age of fourteen. I was not amused. "You know I've been working hard to be willing to stay single for you, so why are you teasing me so?" I complained to God. I couldn't dare to believe anything could come of our encounter and feared I was being led on to be let down.

My family was delighted with Stuart and lost no time in telling me so. I couldn't help being delighted as well but was quite sure this had to be a test—only a test and not the real thing at all (like the emergency warning system on radio). Reality, I told myself sternly, would soon set in, and he would disappear into thin air, leaving my heart broken beyond repair. I prepared for the crunch. Instead it began to dawn on me (incredible thought) that maybe this super young man was actually part of the Big Plan for me.

I had already determined the Big Plan for my life was to please God and serve him with everything I had—to love him supremely, work my head off for his kingdom, and become a wise woman of God. Could it be we could do this together? Be a team? Double trouble for the devil, double blessing for the church, and double joy to each other? I thought about the list, the hands, the figure kneeling by the bed. He knew I was willing. In amazement I began to understand the decision had been made for me. I had chosen to let him choose, and he had chosen. Within one short week we were both convinced that an ongoing relationship was indeed God's idea, and we happily found ourselves on the inside of the Big Plan looking out rather than on the outside looking in!

Stuart shared his own journey toward me. He had not been lacking for girlfriends in the past, but after ending quite a lengthy friendship with a girl, he had told the Lord he would stay uninvolved unless and until he was shown differently. "I'm happy to serve you as a single person," he had said, "but if part of the Big Plan for me is to meet someone who could match my vision and companion me through life, then let me meet her soon. Otherwise you and

I will go it alone." As we shared the timing of his prayer wish and my wish list, we discovered it matched exactly!

We immediately determined that the context of our relationship would be ministry, and that we would nurture the growth of it as we continued the things we were doing for God. It was tempting to stop spending so much time in Christian work and give ourselves a chance to enjoy getting to know each other. Stuart was busy traveling all over England between his job with the bank inspection team and lay preaching on the weekends. Rather than opting out of our commitments, we accompanied each other to the meetings we were both being invited to. We didn't "compartmentalize" our lives, serving God on Sundays and each other Monday through Saturday; rather, we involved ourselves in serving God together all week long. We got to know each other by listening to each other talk to church youth, student groups, Bible studies, and street kids. This way I learned what Stuart believed.

I discovered he believed in a God who was quite big enough for anyone's problems, whatever size they happened to be. I liked that. I listened as he explained that he was a believer, not because it made him feel good, but because he believed with all his heart, mind, and soul that Christianity was true. I really liked that. I sensed an inner compulsion constraining him to preach and teach, telling his world about the urgency of believing the Christian gospel. I loved that! Few things show you more about people than learning what they believe and why they believe it. And so our relationship began to blossom in the fertile field of ministry.

Our few brief visits together were shared with lots of people. We grew to know and love each other as we watched each other minister. When I saw Stuart roughhousing with a kid from my youth group, I thought to myself, *What a fantastic father he will make.* When he made everyone laugh at a banquet with his wonderful sense of humor, I thought, *What marvelous fun we are going to have together.* I knew how intense a person I was and saw at once how his loving teasing would release me from a spiritual uptightness, which I sometimes confused with spiritual uprightness (definitely not helpful to my physical well-being). In other words, he refused to let me take myself too seriously. He made me laugh!

When I had to wait in line to talk to him after he finished speaking, I wasn't impatient or irritated because I was too overwhelmed with a huge sense of privilege. How could God have gifted me with a man like this—a man after his own heart? I was awed and humbled.

"I don't deserve it, Lord," I remember saying.

"Right," he answered, "but I don't give people what they deserve, or they would all be crucified tomorrow. I give my children gifts of grace to enjoy."

I struggled to keep a little part of my heart intact. After all, I reasoned, perhaps Stuart or I would drop dead. (I'm a pretty negative thinker!) Maybe it would be more prudent to make sure I didn't commit all of my affections to him just yet, until we were absolutely sure this was God's will. But apparently my heart wasn't listening again. I knew it was a lost cause. So I decided that C. S. Lewis was right when he wrote in *The Four Loves,* "To love anything, your heart will certainly be wrung and possibly be broken," and I gave up the idea of ever coming out of this particular relationship all in one piece.

In fact, I came to the conclusion that if we had made a mistake it would even be well worth a broken heart. Throwing caution to the winds, I fell totally, helplessly in love.

2
Models of Marriage

Stuart

Jesus once told a man that even though foxes have their holes and birds have their nests he didn't have anywhere to lay his head, to call home. He wasn't complaining—he was explaining. Christ was affirming the normalcy of the desires and the legitimacy of their satisfaction. But he was also admitting that his mission was so demanding that he sometimes denied himself the most basic satisfactions of the most basic desires and needs.

When Mr. Fox returns home after a hard day's hunting he finds his sweet wife, Vixen, waiting. And when Dicky Bird flies home in the evening there is his chirpy little mate out on a limb waiting for him. And from the beginning of time, human beings have instinctively looked for similar situations. Foxes and birds and people have a common longing for belonging: a desire to love and be loved, to appreciate and be appreciated, to accept and be accepted, just to know there is a special person in a special place who has that special ability to make one feel special.

This longing for belonging is caught, not taught—or better, born, not grown. It is as natural as the cry of parched lips for water or the growl of the empty stomach for food. Sad to say, like all things natural it exhibits a crass fallenness at times. All too often it seeks sexual gratification without commitment or a perverted desire for "getting" divorced from "giving." But even the most fallen of us in nobler moments show signs of a search, rich and refined, for a relationship at once physical, emotional, social, and spiritual. Intimacy at many levels—of minds mutually enriched, of emotions mutually matured, of spirits mutually ennobled, of bodies mutually fulfilled.

When Jill and I met we discovered that we had both looked at the possibility of such a relationship long before we ever had the chance to look on each other. But strange to say, neither of us was in any great hurry. Like swimmers lounging by a pool on a hot day, enjoying the anticipation of refreshing coolness before taking the plunge, we were both living fully and well while at the same time anticipating something even fuller and better. We were thoroughly enjoying anticipation on the way to participation. But our anticipation, we discovered later when we compared notes, was not only instinctual but, more accurately, God-imparted. We had been surrounded by models of marriage. We had been exposed to marriages that had matured, relationships that had given us a window into the potential riches of lives shared.

Jill's parents, Bill and Peggy, had a marriage at once comfortable and comforting. When I met them they lived in a beautiful home, drove fine cars, and dined at the best restaurants. They were free in their spending—to the point of extravagance, in comparison to my much more frugal family.

Bill's love of solitude led him to spend endless hours fishing for salmon in season and preparing to fish for salmon out of season. His ambition in life was to own a manor house in the country with its own stretch of salmon river—and he achieved it.

Peggy devoted herself to him, their home, two daughters, and a succession of cocker spaniels. They were quiet people, shy and generous, apparently content to live well in the context of family and a close-knit circle of friends. I rarely heard them disagree, although when Bill announced to Peggy that he had bought her a special furry present for Christmas she, expecting a fur coat, was not exactly ecstatic to discover it was a racehorse! But they learned quickly to laugh about it, even though it not only lost every race but also threatened to lose most of Bill's friends when he persuaded them it was going to win. It was a marriage of devotion without being overtly devout.

They had started out in a simple, humble fashion. Bill, unable or unwilling to get along with his father, struck out on his own as a teenager and soon showed, as he went from house to house fixing things, that he was both a good engineer and an excellent entrepreneur. Peggy had come to Liverpool from her native Scotland as a very young girl and parlayed her homegrown skills into a steady job as a seamstress. From such beginnings they had built a successful business and a reputation for hard work and fair play, straight shooting and transparent integrity. Into such a marriage Jill and her sister, Shirley, were born: a secure home, a solid marriage, and all the perks of material success.

In early days Bill and Peggy had attended a small mission church, and occasionally they talked about a blind preacher and quietly expressed a genuine personal faith. But in the distant past, of which they never spoke in detail, they had been offended, left the fellowship, and never returned. Private in devotion, they declined to be public in practice. But the spiritual roots were there— hidden but deep.

I too had observed firsthand a marriage both secure and sound. It had not only stood the test of time but survived the slings and arrows, if not of outrageous fortune, certainly of extreme testing. My parents, Stanley and Mary, had embarked on a business venture early in their marriage in the depths of the Great Depression. It had never been easy. In later years in the United States I learned the expression "Mom and Pop store" and discovered that was where my early years were spent. In fact, it was really a "Mom, Pop, and kids store" because my brother and I were required to work there, too.

After surviving, barely I think, the Depression, my family, like everybody else's in England in 1939, was hit with the consequences of World War II. This meant that my father, a conscientious objector, was drafted into the Fire Service and my mother was left to run the business and the family. She did both with great skill and success—at least in the business. Those who know my brother, Bernard, and me must feel free to judge the measure of her success in child rearing!

Despite impossible rationing laws, bureaucratic burdens, and rapidly failing health, she carried on and the business grew. At the same time my father was lay-pastoring a tiny church which, like Britain, had its "finest hour" during the war because young men from all over the British Empire were sent to our town for training with the Royal Air Force. Most of the Christians among them, and many who were not, made our home and church their off-base of operations. My parents fed them, housed them, counseled them, wrote their loved ones in faraway places, and frequently corresponded with brokenhearted families whose sons lost their lives in gunfights over Nazi Germany.

My parents were no-nonsense, little-leisure, hard-working, God-fearing, people-serving stalwarts. Tough on the outside, tender inside, they loved the Lord deeply, served him faithfully, and worked tirelessly. If I were an artist, which I am not, I would have painted them standing side by side, shoulder to shoulder, looking resolutely into the distance with firm countenance and gentle eyes, gripping tightly the tools of their trade in one hand and the Scriptures by which they earnestly endeavored to order their lives in the other.

As Jill and I began to realize that our lives were being drawn inexorably toward each other, we began both consciously and subconsciously to look with new eyes on the marriage of our parents—each other's parents, that is. Jill, who was a relatively new believer, felt very keenly the absence of overt spiritual training in her upbringing and was disappointed that there had not been a more open expression of faith in her family life. To be able, therefore, to sit down with my father and talk about the Lord and to go as a family to worship were special treats for her. She was anxious to have a marriage where this sort of thing was normative.

On the other hand, my experience of frugal, disciplined, somewhat spartan Christianity—that regarded sports and entertainment as worldliness to be eschewed, and travel, dining out, and sleek cars as perks of the rich and famous that Christians rarely enjoyed—had left me somewhat frustrated as I had read in the Bible that God gives us all things richly to enjoy. My experience had led me to believe that if God had given us lots of things to enjoy he had omitted to tell my parents, and my efforts to do so had not been well received. So Jill's family was a refreshing change for me! While Jill saw in my parents' marriage things she desired and I took for granted, I saw in her parents' marriage things which she had assumed everybody enjoyed but which I was ready to integrate into my marriage. In other words, we deeply appreciated both models of marriage and were eager to blend what we had observed into our life together.

There were other powerful influences. Jill often talked about families that had opened hearts and homes to her shortly after she came to faith. They had been very sensitive

15

to the needs of this young student and others like her, who needed special spiritual care and nurture. While still in Cambridge, she was invited to spend Sunday afternoons with some former missionaries, their boisterous children, and other students who were encouraged to enjoy a home away from home, a friendly place of meeting with a warm, accepting atmosphere of counseling and care. She knew right away that a home and family like that could make an immense difference in the formative spiritual life of young people, and she knew that she would like to make that kind of home, too, if she ever married.

On one occasion we were invited to conduct a *squash* in the home of a well-known businessman and his wife, Nick and Joy Carr. (A *squash* is an English phenomenon where young people are squashed into a room in which they sit on the floor, sing choruses, and listen to a speaker who sits on the only chair.) Nick was a member of a famous family of manufacturers, and his wife, Joy, was the unflappable mother of their large brood of children. In the middle of the squash the chimney caught on fire, smoke filled the room, the assembled crowd of teenagers coughed and spluttered, and Joy calmly announced, "Oh dear, we seem to have a slight problem. Stuart, you carry on talking. I'll call the fire brigade, and I'm sure everything will be all right."

I looked to her husband for confirmation; he smiled his usual smile, nodded his head vigorously—and we carried on! We survived both fire and squash admirably and after a good night's sleep went downstairs for breakfast with the family.

This too was an experience. Each child (there seemed to be at least ten of them) had his own packet of cereal, which was stacked in the middle of a vast table around which the children sat, stood, squirmed, or screamed in a constant uproar. Until, that is, Father announced that it was time for devotions. Incredibly, a silence that I would never have dreamed possible descended, and for a few, very few, moments the children listened to a brief reading from Scripture, an even briefer explanation of it that I was volunteered to give, prayers from two or three of the kids, and a chorus sung with evident relish if with little musical finesse. Devotions over, the rambunctious family returned to the lively business of growing up.

Driving home, Jill and I compared notes and agreed that the mixture of carefree good humor and serious commitment, noisy freedom and genuine devotion, practical common sense and reckless abandon, not to mention generous hospitality and unaffected friendliness and approachability were the very stuff of marriage and family as far as we were concerned.

Harry and Dorothy Green also were great favorites of ours. Harry, a highly regarded bank manager who had steered me in the direction of a banking career, was a big, blunt, jolly man who was clearly in charge of most situations in which he was to be found. His wife, Dorothy, was quiet by comparison, matter-of-fact, and apparently impervious to stress even though she ran a large household. For all her gentle spirit she was more than a match for her ebullient husband.

One day, to our mingled amazement and amusement, she responded to Harry's good-natured grumbling about something or other with the immortal line, "Harry Green, you had all the world to choose from and you chose me. Now please shut up and be satisfied."

On another occasion the family was entertaining a number of us, including a high-ranking bank official. The four children—all adolescents—had been given strict instructions that they were to be seen and not heard during the meal. Dorothy had made a particular point of explaining that she had grown, picked, and cooked the Brussels sprouts and was for some strange reason, which the family could not comprehend, very pleased with this achievement.

Suddenly Malcolm, their gangly third child, said in a booming voice, "What's this caterpillar doing in my Brussels sprouts?"

To which his father, without missing a beat, said, "Be quiet, boy, and eat your grub." (For the benefit of those who might miss the intended pun, *grub* is another word for *food* in some English circles!) There was no shortage of wit and wisdom, love and laughter in the Green house, and we loved it.

Alf and Barbara Doidge were special people in my life, and I suspect they would never have suspected it. Barbara and my mother had become friends shortly before I was born. The Doidges, who had no children, lived in a small, unpretentious house in the shadow of the forbidding slag heaps (massive, man-made mountains of waste from the mines) that dominated both the landscape and economy of my hometown. Barbara had a loud, contagious laugh that seemed to be in operation in all circumstances. Alf had a quiet, droll sense of humor that was rarely absent. Barbara was an accomplished organist and pianist; Alf, a well-known cricketer for the town team.

They didn't attend the small church that my father "pastored" and, while my parents never really understood this, I like that about them because I know they were *real* and yet didn't fit exactly into our mold. As I had my doubts about some of the exclusiveness of my parents' spirituality, Barbara and Alf gave me confidence to believe that God was bigger than I had been led to believe, and his people came in a variety of shapes and sizes I, as yet, had never seen. Perhaps it was because they had no children of their own that they were so kind to me. They always seemed to have time for me or anyone else who arrived.

Alf loved to sit in his old armchair, contentedly smoking his pipe, solving the daily crossword. Barbara would be in constant motion, laughing, talking, visiting, playing, teaching. While she raised clouds of dust, he puffed clouds of smoke. She gave me my first taste for music; he taught me how to solve crossword puzzles. They were so different but so together, so devoted to each other but so content to give the other space to develop. Music and sports, the neighborhood kids, church choir, and quiet hours by the fire were all parts of what I sensed was a thoroughly happy marriage, and I liked it even as a teenager.

If Alf was playing a game of cricket, Barbara was busy rehearsing a choir piece. If Barbara was tied up teaching piano, Alf was at his workbench making somebody a set of cabinets. When both were free they would roam the countryside for miles, drinking in every tiny detail of nature's wonders. And when they got home Alf toasted crumpets on the open fire grate while Barbara baked a cake, and then quietly they would pray, eat their simple meal, and enjoy just being together. Salt-of-the-earth people, honest, genuine, wonderful, together people. Simple, unaffected, perfectly contented people. Without me being aware of it they were modeling life and marriage to me, and I was all ears and all eyes, and all of fourteen.

None of us can even hope to discover all the factors that have gone into making us the unique persons we have become. And probably no one can identify adequately all the formative ideas about marriage that we carry with us down the aisle. But they are there whether we recognize them or not, and they make a profound impact whether we acknowledge it or not. Jill and I, we soon discovered, had a flying start because of the models of marriage to which we had been exposed. How much we learned from them and to what extent we have benefitted from their examples is a subject we often ponder.

<u>3</u>

"That's That"

Jill

"Let's enjoy every part of our relationship," said Stuart with great enthusiasm. We were discussing our engagement. How long should we wait to get married, we wondered. What was the point of an engagement, anyway? There had to be more to it than diamonds glistening in the sun.

Of course the diamonds were a special part of it for me. What young girl doesn't dream about the romantic moment Romeo proposes and slips the ring on Juliet's finger? And so after deciding the big issues—like the waiting period and just what we would do with it—we decided to attend to the lesser, but nonetheless exciting business of purchasing the symbol of our promises to each other.

The traditional ring in our day was one with three diamonds set in a row. Some people would tend toward the extravagant and buy a solitaire, and others dared to vary the stones a little, but three seemed proper and right for us, not least because we wanted to remember that God was the center of our marriage and Stuart and I were set securely on each side of him. We were all bound up in the bundle of life's experience together by an eternal circle of gold—speaking of the sterling quality of his commitment to us and to our marriage.

The event wasn't quite what I had imagined it would be, however, since it had to fit between Stuart's busy banking and speaking schedule and my teaching responsibilities. And so we found ourselves in downtown Liverpool during rush hour buying the first pretty three-diamond ring we saw.

Never mind, I thought to myself. *I'm sure Stuart will make up for the lack of atmosphere by his Wordsworth-like words as he gives it to me.* I remembered vaguely someone giving a talk about the sort of man Christian girls should look for and saying somewhat severely, "What do you want: character or atmosphere?" Recalling this I couldn't help wondering why a bit of both shouldn't be a possibility!

As we tumbled back to the car through heavy traffic and unwrapped our precious parcel, Stuart gently took my hand and slipped the ring on my third finger. *Here it is,* I thought excitedly.

"Well darling," my brand-new fiance announced emphatically with an extraordinary amount of satisfaction, "that's that!" And believe it or not, that was indeed that! *So much for my romantic, poetic dreams,* I thought to myself. *Never mind, though. I'm sure he'll improve as time goes on.*

Returning home we discovered my mother talking to a friend who sold diamonds. She was busy promising her that we would buy the ring from her. When I flashed my third finger furiously in front of her, my mother pushed the phone into my hand to explain and I stammered, "Oh Mrs. Cappell, I'm so sorry. We've already purchased the ring. But . . . but . . . maybe next time!" My mother disappeared chuckling and I said good-bye as Stuart firmly took the phone out of my hands, replaced it in the cradle, took me in his arms, and said just as enthusiastically and emphatically as the first time—

"There won't be a next time, Jill. Don't you remember I told you—'That's that'?"

And suddenly those two little words became the most romantic, loving, incredible words in the whole wide world!

They spoke of a man who had chosen to be a man of his word and commit himself to me for all time, till death parted us. They told me that while seedtime and harvest, winter and summer, snow and heat continued, he would continue steadfastly loving and cherishing me. Above all they told me I could count on that faithfulness morning and evening—Monday to Sunday, January to December. I wouldn't need to wonder if he was flirting, or wishing he wasn't married to me. It wouldn't matter if we were in the same room or three thousand miles apart; I would be able to thoroughly trust him out of sight. Yes, those two little words were wonderful, and there have been hundreds of times in the intervening years I have repeated them to myself.

Like a couple years ago, for instance. I had just taken a "baby sabbatical," canceling out of everything I could to be available for our daughter's first child and our eldest son's third and fourth—twins! It had been an incredibly hectic time of joy and laughter, sleepless nights and worried moments, but it had also necessitated Stuart and me being apart over Christmas, the only time of the year we could generally count on being together. Then after one short day together Stuart had boarded a plane to Saudi Arabia and I to Holland—actually from the very same airport but different gates. But "that's that," you see. Our commitment spans thirty-five years, so much of it in separate spheres of service to the Lord, but always undergirded by our personal and utter confidence in each other.

Christ being the center and circumference of our marriage has meant time spent apart, as he has sent us to speak to the four corners of the globe. Few have been the times we have joyfully found ourselves in the same corner, but Christ centered in our hearts and home has meant his enabling power to keep those commitments we made to each other when we got engaged. After all, Jesus died on the cross, rose from the dead, and said, "That's that" for us. There was an eternal finality about his commitment. His risen life imparts to us his faithfulness to follow through on our commitments also.

And so our engagement began with a ring that has spoken of the centrality of Christ every day since. It reminds us both of our total commitment to him and therefore our total commitment to each other. When Christ is central he helps us to be faithful people. That is the key.

So thirty-five years ago Stuart decided we would give ourselves time to enjoy our new status: engagement. He said he believed that a suitable period should be given to enjoy and explore this new experience—learning to be sure about each other's affections. This would be our opportunity to learn in safety how to disclose ourselves fully to each other. Seeing that we were now living in the context and in anticipation of a lifetime of total and faithful commitment, we could relax and not be afraid something either of us discovered would make any difference. Engagement, in other words, was a safe place to learn the good and the bad, the things we liked and the things we didn't about each other—the joys and the surprises.

What would Stuart think of me, for instance, when he learned I was such a worrier, I worried! Maybe being so very positive a person himself, he would be quite disgusted with such an apparent lack of faith on my part. But even though I worried about it, I felt a freedom to talk it out because of my new sense of security. I was living in the good of a promise, you see. Even though I'm sure my future husband was a little surprised to discover I would worry up worries no one had ever thought of worrying up before, he worked happily at trying to balance my negative train of thought with a caboose of fun and faith that changed my winters into spring.

Giving ourselves time in the engagement period afforded us lots of lessons to respond rather than react to each other's idiosyncrasies. We had refused to use our precious parenthesis between singleness and the married state to rob us of this by cluttering it up with wedding details. These we kept at bay and didn't allow to intrude until we'd tasted the blessings of our betrothal to the full.

We found that our engagement also gave us a chance to talk about our dreams and to plan our future. How exciting to discover that our dreams matched! Stuart talked about having a home where other people's children would want to come. Having both been involved with teenagers in volunteer youth work, we knew how important it was for them to come into the loving, accepting atmosphere of a Christian home. Then we had the models of the friends who had showered us with loving hospitality. We talked about the sort of home we'd make together. I wondered a little about the furnishings and if I'd be able to cook nice enough meals to entertain, but as we began to talk about it all, I realized the kids wouldn't be coming to see my drapes or sample the cake I had made, but would come because they wanted to meet the Christ we knew. They would come because they knew Jesus lived with us. Now we were excited! Yes, we agreed, we would let it be known we had an open-door policy as well as open ears and hearts for any of them who needed to talk over their worries and fears, hopes, aspirations, or problems. Our house, unlike the post office, would not have hours.

We dreamed about where we would live and whether Stuart would continue his career in the bank or maybe leave it behind for the privilege of some full-time Christian employment. His time was already full with many, many opportunities to preach in local churches and youth groups, and the flow of invitations showed no signs of abating. Where would we end up? we thought excitedly. Would God lead him to have a Christian presence in the business world, or to be a busy full-time servant in Christian work? Either way, our eyes brightened at the potential prospects.

We shared our personal struggles, too. We talked about how we had come to terms with our singleness, as we decided to wait for the "right" partner and God's go-ahead before we committed ourselves to any more boy-girl relationships. We had both decided if we were to get involved at all it would have to be with one who wanted, above everything else, to love and serve the Lord. We had both determined to choose nothing less than a fully committed Christian partner. It would not be enough, we had decided, to settle for "a Christian" because he or she was "a Christian," but rather a deep Christian, a consistent Christian, an excited Christian.

I well remember the day we opened our Bibles together and shared a special verse that God had given us both in this regard. What a thrill when each of us turned to the very same verse—heavily underlined in each of our Bibles:

"As for me and my house, we will serve the LORD" (Joshua 24:15, KJV).

I told Stuart about my struggle to remain willing to be single and how after eventually giving that struggle to God, I had come across Joshua's words "Choose for yourselves this day whom you will serve." Having chosen, I read on to what has since become our verse—"As for me and my house, we will serve the LORD." I had no idea if there was to be a "we" at all, I explained, but I determined I would serve him anyway with or without a partner.

God would be my focus, my center, my balance, my vision, and my friend. He would be my companion, my highest joy and my deepest purpose, my all-consuming passion. When, and if, God would choose to give me a husband with the same goals, we together would surely double that energy and ministry for him.

Stuart talked about the family we might have, and we let our minds race ahead to the incredible blessing and miracle of little eternal people in the shape of boys or girls. "I'd want our kids to be part of it all," Stuart said. "Oh yes," I echoed excitedly. "The text says, 'As for me and my house, we will serve the LORD.' I don't want to watch you doing it, without doing it myself," I told my fiance. "And I'm sure you don't want to watch me doing my thing while you twiddle your thumbs. What's more, I'm doubly convinced we don't want our kids standing passively on the sidelines cheering us both on." We agreed we wanted the whole family caught up in the glorious possibilities of serving Christ together.

Somehow we knew instinctively then that the art of Christian parenting was finding the secret of serving him together, with each special person in the family doing his or her part and consequently feeling totally necessary and valuable to the whole process. We had absolutely no idea as to what was involved, but we both knew we wanted it—badly. Badly enough to make it happen.

And so our engagement became a wide place—a grand place, a deep place to discover how God had planted the same desires in each of our hearts, and to talk about how to realize these dreams.

Engagement also became a place to begin discovering our very great differences. They say opposites attract, and in Stuart's and my case, that certainly was true. As we invested time getting to know each other, each new facet of the other's personality was a delightful and sometimes startling surprise. I found out Stuart was laid-back, relaxed, lots and lots of fun, and very bright—especially with figures. On the other hand, I was uptight, found having fun hard, had a negative attitude even on Fridays, and had given up on math around the age of fourteen. How could two such diverse people fall in love? Engagement for us was a means of "engaging" to understand some of these differences and to try to accept them.

I overheard a north country Englishman commenting to a friend on the uncertainty of marriage. He said somewhat skeptically, "You never know what you've got until you've got them home and the door shut!" I smiled, but I didn't totally agree. Giving time before marriage took care of a lot of surprises and presented a chance to work out some of the difficulties. Initially opposites do attract, but it's also a well-known fact that, once married, opposites can irritate. We found that our engagement gave us a chance to deal with some of that irritation and the clashes that resulted, without marring the young marriage.

Above all, our engagement gave us a chance to begin to pray together. We were to discover prayer to be as strong a glue in our relationship as service would be. Somehow prayer shut us up with God and his warmth and the peace of his presence. When we prayed together we were enveloped in the circle of God's arms. And after spending time close to him, we ended up feeling closer to each other! But we also learned we mustn't substitute our prayers together for our prayers alone. Both must happen. Both were extremely important. Both were totally necessary. I was to learn in the years that lay ahead that prayer would bring Stuart, who may well be twelve thousand miles away, closer than breathing. In the chamber of prayer the God who listens to us both spans the globe with a glance and diminishes the distance to nothing. I could "travel" to Africa, India, South America, or wherever my husband happened to be and "be there" with him.

So during our engagement we promised to pray for each other every single day, a "that's that" commitment both of us have succeeded in keeping. There is no question in my mind that prayer seals promises, grows love and awareness of the other's needs, and works to promote harmony.

As we enjoyed our betrothal we took our first delightful steps in "family" prayer—investing in eternal habits that would last our whole life through. After what we felt was an adequate period of time, it became the appropriate thing to do to begin planning the wedding. We had some memories to keep now. A part of our love story was safely wrapped up, labeled engagement, and stored safely in our hope chest—thought on with affection, and remembered with thanksgiving and gratitude.

So my mother, Peggy, and I set about finding a beautiful white wedding dress—high at the collar and old-fashioned lace—a dress that I later was able to give to a beautiful German girl on our mission team for her wedding, who handed it on to a Christian girl, behind the Iron Curtain in Poland, who couldn't afford one either. How wonderful to give a special part of our day of days to other girls who wanted to establish Christian homes, too, and who otherwise would never have been able to purchase such a lovely dress.

We shopped, made lists, wrote invitations, and received presents (usually given before the wedding in England). We were presented with thirty-two tablecloths in all! We had no showers in England, as it wasn't considered proper etiquette to make a list and ask for things. So people had to do their best to guess, and in our case thirty-two of them all guessed the same.

Trying desperately to think of something new to say in the way of appreciation at the appearance of the thirty-second tablecloth, I took it out of my employer's hands with the words, "Oh Miss Marsh, how sweet of you. As you can see, we already have many that are far too nice to use, but this one will be wonderful for everyday." Needless to say, this did not endear me to my head teacher!

We couldn't believe so many things needed doing, but Peggy and my sister, who was to be my maid of honor, tackled it all in a typically efficient manner. They spoiled me, leaving me with the fun stuff. At last the day approached, and Stuart and I faced it with joy and anticipation. God was about to join us together.

4

Here Comes the Bride—But Where's the Bridegroom?

Stuart

As a small boy I used to insist that I had attended my parents' wedding. The obvious embarrassment my insistence caused my parents was not obvious to me because the thought of them doing anything without me was most disconcerting. But I assure you of this, I did not attend their wedding. In fact I cannot remember attending anybody's wedding before my own, although it is quite possible I did. Evidently they were eminently forgettable. Since that time, of course, I have attended possibly hundreds of weddings, most of them in the capacity of presiding minister. Now I may be something of an expert, but on my own big day I was a total neophyte.

Young people getting married in our church today are required to attend our premarital class, take personality profiles, and meet with the pastor who will officiate at the wedding. My preparation for my wedding day came from my mother-in-law elect, who told me, "Just get yourself there on time!"

In fact, my premarital counseling was more or less on the same level. It came from my father-in-law elect, who, when I asked him if I could marry Jill, said with a mildly surprised expression, "Of course you can." Then after a pause he sighed and said, "I think we're supposed to talk, aren't we?"

"I've no idea," I replied. "I've never done this before."

To which he replied, "Well, all you need to remember is, don't expect anything logical." Having said that, he heaved a sigh of relief, his marriage counseling responsibilities fulfilled, and sat back with a satisfied look on his face. I didn't know whether he meant that marriage isn't logical or that he didn't regard his daughter as logical, and I didn't want to ask. So we just sat there in silence for a while and then, to the relief of both of us, we changed the subject. (Incidentally, subsequent events have proved quite conclusively that he was referring to his daughter when he advised against expecting anything logical!)

From my point of view there wasn't anything very logical in the meeting Bill and I were having together. Jill and her mother had decided that I should formally approach Bill and ask for the hand of his daughter. The date was arranged, but then a problem arose. I had contracted some kind of septic infection and blood poisoning that kept me in bed in the Manchester YMCA hostel, which was home at that time. I had suggested to Jill that since I could not stand up, let alone travel to Liverpool, we should plan my "approach" when I could do it in manly fashion, standing on my own two feet.

But that was too logical for Jill. So she arrived at the YMCA, recruited two strong, young men, who hauled me out of bed, helped me dress, and then carried me out to the car in an armchair. I don't remember how I was maneuvered out of the car at the other end, but I do remember being placed tenderly on a couch and wrapped in blankets to await my father-in-law elect, who had used the delay in my arrival as an excuse to go to his club for his evening libation.

> ◼◀◼◀◼◀◼

But now the big day had arrived. We had met briefly with the minister the evening before. It had been a little strained because Jill had gotten herself in the middle of a church controversy. She had been asked to work with the church young people, which she had eagerly agreed to; but as she already had quite a crowd of youngsters in tow who never went to church, she had the great idea of integrating them.

In theory this is the way to go; in practice it's a little problematic. At that time, the church-growth experts had not invented the terms *heterogeneous* and *homogeneous* to describe the fact that some folks just won't mix with others, and you'd better believe it! Matters came to a head when one of Jill's "converts" helped himself to a gold cigarette lighter from the pocket of the chairman of the board and when he was caught simply said, "In your position you shouldn't have one of these anyway!" A remark which, while it probably contained more than a grain of truth, did nothing to help strained relations with the board. It all culminated in them asking Jill kindly to take her kids else-where shortly before the wedding. Anyway, we made polite conversation with the minister for a little while and de-parted—somewhat different from the elaborate rehearsals I have gone through on many a Friday night since that time.

My brother, my parents, and I stayed overnight in a hotel—that in and of itself being quite an event for my family in those days. We (the men that is) had rented the traditional "toppers and tails" and Royal Ascot outfit favored for weddings. I remember waking early, eating a vast breakfast, and then realizing there was still a lot of time before I "got myself to the church on time." So I decided to clean the car. I don't ever remember having such an urge before or since, but on that occasion it seemed the thing to do.

Unfortunately, I must have become so engrossed in my task that I misjudged the time and barely made it to the church before Jill. On hearing of this later my brand-new mother-in-law expressed her displeasure quietly but firmly, concluding with a self-conscious giggle and pointing to her cheek indicating exactly where she wanted a kiss to show that we loved each other anyway (a ritual which over the years became a normal part of our special relationship). After my brother and I left for the church my parents decided that they had been forgotten so my father, resplendent in his wedding garments, rushed into the street in front of a car, flagged it down, and asked the startled driver if he would mind very much taking them to their son's wedding. He obliged and they arrived safely, if a little flustered. Meanwhile the limousine driver who had been dispatched to the hotel to transport them started a search for the missing parents of the groom who were happily sitting in the church oblivious to the consternation outside.

As we got ready to enter the church I couldn't help thinking about the psalmist who compared the sun to a bridegroom leaving his chamber like a "strong man to run a race," and while I wouldn't have described myself in such terms, I was eager to get on with the task at hand. I was certainly more interested in the thought of being married than the wedding process whereby I would achieve that noble estate. But I had to admit the idea of attending my own wedding had terrific appeal.

Naturally, I was most interested in seeing Jill. She, her mother, and her sister had been busy for what seemed to be months preparing for the event. I had no idea what they could have been doing, but I knew that no effort would have been spared to make a beautiful bride. Little did I imagine that Jill, resplendent in all her wedding finery, standing in the middle of the room on a dust sheet to protect her dress from all stains and ready far too early, had developed a fit of nerves. The "heebie-jeebies" we call them in England. The symptoms, apparently, were deathly pallor of the countenance, total rigidity of the limbs, and tearful articulation of the inability to proceed. Her father, quiet at the best of times and not expecting anything logical, stood by helpless, clad in toppers and tails, wishing he was standing up to his middle in a salmon river, matching wits with fish rather than trying to understand daughters. Jill's mother, Peggy, ever the practical one, overlooking her staunch teetotalism in the crisis, said, "Bill, give her a shot of brandy!" At the thought of arriving at her nuptials with alcohol on her breath, Jill was instantly cured of whatever ailed her, climbed into the waiting limousine, and headed for the church.

Her dad, she insists, did not say a single word to her on the trip, and we will never know his thoughts. Years later, when I was in a similar position with Judy, our daughter, I recalled what my friend Jay Kesler had told me about giving his daughter away. He told me that when he saw that great big fellow waiting for his sweet little daughter, he thought it was like giving a Stradivarius to a gorilla. I had shared this with Judy prior to her wedding day and reminded her of it as we started down the aisle. No wonder people were surprised to see us both laughing so heartily while stepping so majestically. I must, however, admit that as I went further into the service for Judy I began to choke up (emotions play tricks at weddings). I suspect on my own wedding day that Bill, a quiet, reserved man, was battling his emotions in the best British "stiff upper lip" tradition. He had never been given to hugs and kisses and terms of endearment, preferring rather to show his love for his girls in generous gifts and the best of everything.

When I told him some time later that I was leaving the bank to enter the ministry, he responded shyly, "I know the Lord will care for you, but be assured that as long as I'm alive you'll never lack anything." I knew him well enough to know it was true. No doubt he was dreading having to walk the aisle and stand at the front of the church, and he may even have been thinking back to the days when he regularly attended public worship and taught a Bible class. Perhaps he was even contemplating the fact that Jill and I seemed bent on following a lifestyle of overt witness, which he had formerly followed before settling for a quieter, more private, less active faith.

This was certainly on Jill's mind because she had repeatedly expressed her desire that the wedding be not only a time when God joined us together but also a proclamation and celebration of the Lord himself, whom we were convinced had brought us together in his own good time in order that we might serve him acceptably in the spheres of influence he had eternally ordained for us.

On arriving at the church Jill's limousine was surrounded by the kids from her youth group—the ones whom she had been asked by the church leaders to take elsewhere. Totally unabashed by this rejection, they had arrived at the church for the wedding, not exactly dressed for the occasion (given that they never went to occasions, they probably didn't own anything suitable). "Three cheers for Jill," they shouted as she emerged from the back seat smiling and suddenly relaxed by the presence and familiarity of her beloved kids. "Oh, doesn't she look smashing!" they enthused, and then with much chattering and clattering they followed her into the church and squashed themselves into the vacant pews.

I didn't know if it was the presence of these kids or the unusual experience of the church being packed to the rafters, but the minister now began to look somewhat unnerved. Sweat began to form on his forehead, his upper lip began to twitch, and a definite tremor was evident as he began to intone, "Dearly beloved brethren—we are gathered here in the presence of God and this company to join together this man and this woman in matrimony." Perhaps, seeing his discomfort, Jill's mother was thinking, *Bill, give him a shot of brandy!*—but he managed okay, and in a remarkably short time "this man" and "this woman" were joined together.

Sad to relate, I have no recollections of the actual service, but I do know that the vows we made to each other before God and the congregation were real and lasting. We were living in a day and age when marriages were built to last. I don't think I had ever met a divorced person at that time. So "till death us do part" was what we said and what we meant and what to this day, more than thirty-five years later, we are still committed to. After being pronounced man and wife Jill and I allowed ourselves a deep private look and a shy, knowing smile. But this was a British wedding. No self-respecting minister who wanted to keep his job would have even thought of the customary American instruction "You may kiss the bride." My mother's reaction when she saw this for the first time in an American wedding was wide-eyed incredulity and a muttered, "Disgusting!"

I don't know how they did it, but the kids managed to get outside the church before we did, so we were bombarded with handfuls of rice thrown with great force and accuracy.

Discretion was clearly the better part of valor so we headed for the limousine and, safely inside, began our married life together. Laughing but close to tears, serious but strangely elated, excited but vaguely apprehensive, spiritually moved yet physically aware of each other as never before, we cherished the few moments together before facing the crowds at the reception.

In British weddings there is a set procedure for formal speeches. The best man—in my case my brother, Bernard—proposes a toast to the bridesmaids that usually degenerates into something resembling a roast of the bridegroom. The bridegroom responds on their behalf and takes time to defend himself and delivers a few well-aimed shots of his own. Then the father of the groom toasts the bride and groom and the bride's father responds. As my brother, father, and I were all lay preachers, we had no problem putting our speeches together, although in retrospect they must have sounded like a triple-header sermon to those who were not used to church. It must have seemed odd to some of these folks that we drank toasts of nothing stronger than orange juice—a decision that had caused a little friction because Bill, who was paying for the reception, couldn't imagine a wedding reception without "appropriate" beverages and worried what his friends would think of him treating them so shabbily (Jill and I were strongly convinced a nonalcoholic celebration was most appropriate). Bill reluctantly conceded the point—I suspect with more grace and sensitivity than that with which we had enforced the point.

He'd also made it clear that wild horses would not get him on his feet to make a speech. But a friend of his agreed to speak, saying among other things that when he'd heard that Jill was marrying a banker who doubled as an evangelist he was terrified. But when he met me and saw that I looked more like a cruiser weight in training and was a former Marine commando to boot, he felt a lot better. He added that when he'd seen our work with kids he'd become a fan and he wished us "God's best"—encouraging words from a self-professed atheist.

✦✦✦✦✦

Shortly thereafter I made the first major mistake of my marriage. There may have been one or two minor infractions in the preceding two or three hours of our marital experience, but if they had happened they promptly paled in comparison to what I did just then. During the course of our friendship and engagement we had been separated by distance and commitments but had bridged the gap with regular phone calls and letters. It's amazing how much engaged couples can find to share in long phone calls and even longer letters, particularly when you realize how little the same couples tend to share a few years into marriage.

Anyway, to get back to my mistake. Now that we were safely married I didn't see any need to keep the letters that Jill had sent to me, so I went up to the room where she was getting ready for our honeymoon trip. The door was slightly ajar, and Jill, who was changing clothes, heard me coming and hastened to close the door. Whereupon the young teenager, who along with Jill's sister constituted Jill's bridesmaid corps, burst out laughing and said, "Jill, you're married to the man, you know." This was not the mistake!

Eventually I was allowed into the room, and, handing the neat stack of letters to Jill, I said, "Here are your letters, Jill. I just wanted to check with you before I threw them away." The bridesmaids gasped, Jill went pale, and then to my intense amazement and embarrassment she burst into tears. Approximately three hours into my marriage I had made my wife cry! I looked helplessly at the bridesmaids, who rushed to Jill's side, making conciliatory noises and looking at me as if I'd crawled out from under a rock. Personally, I would have preferred to find a rock under which I could crawl.

Eventually, Jill said quietly, "You must do whatever you wish with my letters. I'll always keep the ones you sent to me." There was no recrimination in her voice, just hurt. For the first time as a married man my pragmatic maleness had trampled my wife's gently sensitive femaleness. I wish I could say that I promptly learned sensitivity to another's feelings as a result of that devastating episode, but I'm afraid when it comes to that sort of thing I've tended to be a slow learner.

The bridesmaids, having helped to restore the bride's fractured composure, quietly exited the room, and we were left alone for a few moments to do what you do when you've either hurt or been hurt. I assured Jill that I had no idea the letters were so important, that I had simply been trying to clean out my room and was rather pleased with myself that I hadn't just thrown them away but had thought to ask her first. She said she was sorry that she was so weepy and sentimental and she was sure that I was being very sensible and she very silly. But I assured her that the converse was true. After two or three goings-around at this rate we suddenly heard each other, started laughing, and said we were sorry. Jill kept the letters and still has them somewhere to this day.

As the years have rolled by, the misunderstandings have dropped off. We have not always resolved them as quickly as the notorious original on our wedding day, but the steps we took to address the first problem are the same steps we take today. We keep an eye open for the telltale signs of hurt we can easily recognize. We communicate with each other on the subject, which means we tell each other what we think and how we feel and listen carefully to what is being said. We respond as honestly as we can, accepting responsibility for whatever we are convinced we have done. We genuinely apologize and invariably accept each other's apologies, then turn our attention to something positive and pleasant. Then we get on with life.

And that is exactly what we did as we climbed into our little, light gray Austin A35—Bill and Peggy's wonderful wedding present—and headed off into the sunset—or more accurately, down south, enroute to the Continent and our honeymoon.

5

"I Married a Stranger"

*G*etting married does something for you," my brand-new husband told me, grinning appreciatively. "Your eyes are sparkling!" I didn't doubt it. I couldn't help wondering how happy one could be without exploding with the joy of it all.

I had carefully changed out of my wedding dress into my going-away suit, complete with the obligatory hat worn by British brides in those days. I had had a considerable problem finding suitable headgear, as I seldom wore any, but had settled on what I thought was a lovely pink cloche with a huge rose on the front. I was a little startled to discover Stuart wasn't as impressed with it as I was. I think he compared it to a miner's helmet or some such thing, and I remember thinking, *Now how do I cope with such remarks?* When you have been single for a while and used to choosing your own clothes, it's a big change suddenly to have someone who comments so candidly on your attire.

The next night, I suggested Stuart wear a certain tie with his new suit. He said, "I've always chosen my own ties." We looked at each other. He didn't like my hat, and I didn't care for his tie. Could such minor things cause problems on a honeymoon, or more importantly, in a marriage?

We realized that a lifelong adjustment had just begun. We were about to begin to evaluate the importance of our many differences. Did our marriage mean my husband could be rude about my hat and I could clean out his tie rack—was that what it was all about? Or rather, was marriage about learning to appreciate and respect the other's taste and choices, learning to be a little gentler with our criticisms, downgrading them into suggestions?

We had felt we knew each other pretty well, but twenty-four hours had hardly gone by before we began to realize we had both married a stranger. What did I really know about Stuart, I wondered pensively. Why, I didn't even know he felt strongly about choosing his own ties! What would happen when the really important revelations began?

And what did Stuart really know about me? Was he aware I had to sleep on the left side of the bed, hated really cold weather, and felt compelled to read my Bible at exactly the same time every day? I didn't care when I ate my meals or even if I ate them; I found out Stuart felt very strongly about eating his meals exactly on time. He read his Bible at any given moment during the day and could pray on the run; I had to find a "desert island" before I could concentrate on the Lord. My man loved to travel and keep moving; I liked to "nest," or stay put. Stuart stayed totally relaxed even when things were chaotic around him, while I got thoroughly uptight even before I opened my eyes in the morning. Yes, we both decided, each of us had indeed married a stranger.

But then we discovered that this was what a honeymoon was for . . . to begin to intimately introduce ourselves at every level of our beings. And the new things we were about to learn about each other were intended to be a delight and not a distress. We were meant to respond to each other, not to react; to accept the differences, not to set out on an instant crusade to change them—unless, of course, there was an important enough reason.

Take my driving, for instance. I have to admit that was an important enough reason for change. My husband is a brave man, a tough man. I have seldom seen him fazed in situations except when I get behind the wheel of a car and he is with me. Then I see something very akin to fear in his eyes. We set out on our honeymoon to tour Europe—our wedding gift from my parents—in the little Austin car they had given us to accomplish our goal.

The first time Stuart suggested I take the wheel, we were traveling through beautiful Switzerland, approaching the city of Berne.

"Do you want to take a turn driving?" my happy husband inquired cheerfully.

"Yes, I'd like to," I replied.

We swapped places and set off at a great pace. We could go faster in Europe than in England, and I enjoyed the speed and the feeling of power it gave me. Stuart began reminding me we were on the wrong side of the road and needed to watch out and perhaps go a little slower.

"The roundabouts are the worst," he said, beginning to look a little nervous. "You need to remember to go the opposite way round them." No sooner had he said this than we entered Berne. Trying to adjust to everything being reversed, I was suddenly aware of a roundabout looming ahead.

"Watch out now," Stuart warned me sharply, "keep your eyes open for traffic from the left and the right, and be aware of the pedestrians, and drive the speed of the traffic." I began to panic, trying to remember to do everything he told me at once. Glancing at Stuart, I noticed his face was more than a little tense. What was more, his knuckles were white. Now that wasn't necessary, I thought. As I temporarily took my eyes off the road to look at him, we reached the roundabout. I thought I had maneuvered around it quite well until I heard my husband choke, "Jill, I suggest you pull over and let the poor man off the bonnet of the car!"

I looked out the windscreen, and there was this man spreadeagled over the front of the car, clutching the mascot, waving his umbrella and briefcase futilely in the air. I couldn't stop. I realized the man was riding with us because it was the only alternative he had to being run over. And even though I was appalled at his dilemma, I was also nonplussed to know what to do about it. However could I stop to let him off when I was hemmed in with cars that were forcing me to keep moving? And so we all journeyed along together for a while until he suddenly slid off the nose of our car onto the street!

Stuart gazed anxiously backward in time to see the man pick himself up unscathed and walk hurriedly off into the crowd. Naturally I was very anxious about him, too, and so I tried to see what was happening by peering in the driving mirror.

Settling back to the job at hand, I couldn't help but notice the strange behavior of a man on a bicycle just in front of us.

"My," I said to Stuart, "don't these Swiss people bike fast."

"Not really," my husband replied icily. "Only when you somehow get the front bumper of the car hooked under their back mudguard!"

Sure enough, I had managed to do just that. I have no idea how it happened, but the poor man's legs were quite a blur as he was propelled along at "my insistence." Eventually I was able to disengage and allow the man to retreat safely to the side of the road. Seeing he didn't speak English, I couldn't tell him how badly I felt even though I tried. At last he feebly waved us away, and Stuart grimly but firmly took over the wheel. I wondered if my husband would ever let me drive again.

I had no doubt Stuart had expected me to drive well. After all, I was the daughter of a car dealer, and my sister was involved in road racing. Family tradition pointed to my having inherited these abilities. But my driving was terrible, and I have to confess it's never radically improved. Few of my friends feel comfortable about driving with me.

Later that day, lying on a beautiful beach in Italy, I felt vaguely troubled and unsettled. Maybe, I thought, Stuart would expect me to be a wonderful cook. His mother was one of the world's best. What would happen when he was unpleasantly awakened to the realization that my cooking was about as disastrous as my driving? I was pretty sure he wouldn't take over the kitchen like he had taken over the wheel of the car. Whatever would we do? Would he love me less? Would he love me for me or for what I did or didn't do well? In other words, would I need to perform to please?

Honeymoons give people a chance to translate such troubling thoughts into words. It took courage to say to my new husband, "Do you mind me learning on you? I've hardly ever cooked a thing." I'm sure it took a great deal of grace for him to respond cheerfully, "That's fine, Jill. Everyone has to start somewhere." Of course we were on holiday, taking our meals in lovely restaurants at the time, so it was obviously easy to talk about it in such a light fashion. We were both old enough to realize, however, that reality would hit when we got home and the honeymoon was over.

"This is where our relationship to Christ will make the difference," Stuart said confidently. "He'll give us help to sort it out when we have a hard time with each other."

I hoped God was practical and personal enough to bother with such things as my bad driving. Surely he had enough on his mind without us distracting him with such trivial matters. Yet even as I allowed this doubt to creep in, I knew that Christ was indeed interested in the little conflicts of relationships, if for no other reason than that he knew big conflicts grow out of little ones. If we could only learn to work out the small things as soon as they appeared and not sit on them or pretend they weren't happening, we would know what to do with the big ones.

We had been told we were to present ourselves at a home in Austria and collect our honeymoon money gift. We duly arrived and were treated to a delightful welcome, delicious refreshment, and an inside look at a picture-postcard log cabin nestled among the incredible snow-capped Alps. The log cabin was embroidered with window boxes of vibrant color containing flowers with a fragrance you could smell a mile away. It was too easy. All we had to do was arrive, identify ourselves, ask for the money that my father had deposited with these friends for us, and walk out with it in our hands. Then it was up to us to spend it! We had been told not to come home with the change. In fact, my father had been so generous we realized the money would have to be squandered rather than spent.

What a parallel to spiritual wealth in terms of God's gracious and bountiful power and help that he has deposited in Christ for those who believe. He has done his part. He has offered us this treasure—Jesus in our hearts. The rest is up to us. All we need to do is to present ourselves in prayer to our heavenly Father, identify ourselves as sinners Jesus died for and forgave, and hold out our spiritual hands for all the power we need to live and love. Christ is our wealth. We have been made rich beyond our wildest imaginings. It is up to us to appropriate what has been made available in grace. Our heavenly Father invites us to spend, yes, squander his endowment—and tells us not to come home with the change.

"What an advantage we have," I told my husband. "It doesn't seem fair."

"Gifts aren't usually given because it's fair," replied my husband. "Gifts are given irrespective of whether you deserve them or not. Let's just make sure we use all the things the Lord has made available to us in our relationship."

We spent a week in Italy, a week touring, and finished up at the World's Fair in Belgium. I had traveled a good bit on the Continent with my family, but for Stuart it was the first time. We kept moving; he wanted to see as much as he could of as much as there was! It was exhausting, exciting, and exhilarating.

"Why not fill our precious three weeks to the full?" he asked me. "Let's spend—no, squander—our happiness on each other." And so we set off into the wild blue yonder.

It was hot. We stopped our little gray car at the side of a long French road, bought a melon off a fruit stall, and buried our faces in the refreshing red stuff. Stuart had a cocky hat on his head, shorts and sandals, and topped it all off with the biggest grin. He looked totally relaxed—and was. We reveled in the freedom and adventure of belting along unknown roads to unknown destinations.

Of course I spiritualized it all. I gazed at the road ahead and composed poems in my head about the significance of it—while Stuart began to watch the gauge and look for a gas station.

"How can you be so pragmatic?" I asked him.

"How would you like to walk that long, long road in this heat?" he countered practically.

We marveled at the beautiful French fields rolled out flat against the earth like giant heirloom quilts. We climbed through Austria's incredible mountain ranges piercing the low clouds and reminding us of so much white hair on ancient heads. We stayed in little Italian villages so stifling hot we had to fill the bath with cold water to try and cool our blood down to a normal temperature. At night we listened to what seemed to be the entire youth population gunning their motor bikes just outside our window, and in the day we escaped to the long white beaches and peacock blue water, to fry our British skins a blushing pink, then raw red, and eventually as brown as berries.

We ate the strange, exciting food cooked in oil, wine, and goodness knows what else, and giggled and guessed our way through menus that made no sense at all. One day we phoned my parents from the middle of the fabulous Black Forest in the southland of Germany.

"Where are you, darling?" inquired my mom excitedly.

"In the Black Forest," I replied.

There was a moment's silence, then—"Keep away from those Russians," she advised.

Since my geography was as meager as my mother's I promised her we would and hung up.

"Jill, we're miles away from those Russians," Stuart said in amazement. He, I discovered, loved geography—I couldn't even spell it. One more difference to discover, debate, and delight in.

"How fun," I said to him. "You can fill me in on all that geography, and I can spiritualize things like French roads for you." I couldn't imagine how life could be very interesting for him—looking for gas stations instead of composing spiritual parallels about our environment.

It was amazing to me that Stuart could be so spiritually practical. I loved his earthy Christianity: "faith with boots on" as he was one day to describe it. His biblical knowledge wore street clothes and not rich vestments. He devoted himself to making truth talk everyone's language. The

Bible was a totally natural part of his spiritual life. No churchy trappings here. This was very refreshing to me, especially as I seemed to live my life in "another realm," and needed firm anchoring to the ground.

We were to use that glorious three-week vacation as an environment for telling secrets. Hidden things we had hugged to our hearts till now—timid in our desire to make ourselves vulnerable by offering such feelings and thoughts to another. Now there weren't enough minutes in the day to dig down deep inside our treasuries and present our very selves little by little to each other. Soon we would be back at work and our chance to give each other our total, undivided attention would be interrupted.

But even that prospect looked different to us both. Life was manageable now, for there were two of us to manage it. Life was different now, for there were two of us seeing it differently; and we were to discover that would change our whole perspective. And life was bigger now, a wider space to live in, a larger opportunity—because two are better than one at doubling up to take full advantage of life's advantages. We believed two could double the joy, double the possibilities, and make a double dent in the devil's territory. *One of us can chase a thousand, but two will put ten thousand to flight,* I reminded myself.

The World's Fair in Belgium was a fitting and significant ending to our honeymoon, and the beginning of our marriage and ministry proper. How could we possibly know that the world showcased at that fair would be our parish, and that most of the countries represented in Brussels would be countries one or both of us would visit in the cause of Christ within the next thirty years? We wandered from exhibition to exhibition, and came upon staff members of the Billy Graham organization who were showing their films in a tent. It was fun to meet fellow believers and hear of their effective ministry efforts in that world marketplace. We looked around at the ethnic mix of visitors and realized there wasn't a country on the globe that didn't need to hear and understand the great good news of Jesus and his love. We were ready to be part of the team, getting the message out: part of the prayer power making it happen; part of God's whole church, taking the whole gospel to the whole world.

In the midst of all the love and fun and happiness of our honeymoon, we talked much of our ministry together. How could we help each other, support each other, encourage each other, and challenge each other to be all that we should be for him—whom we both so loved and served? How would we choose a church to attend or a people group to serve? Would my role change now that I was married? Would I do more ministry or less now that I was a wife? Would I work in or outside of the home?

We found that honeymoons are times when you reach for the stars together and find the Milky Way at your feet! *The sky's the limit,* my heart insisted, and we turned our little gray car toward Liverpool—our first home, and our first experience of newly married life.

Safely home again, we moved into my parents' home for a few months because the accommodation provided by

Stuart's firm wasn't ready for us. This was the sort of arrangement that marriage experts strongly advise against. However, this particular couple hadn't read their advice or been to their seminars, and we weren't one whit threatened or intimidated with the idea. Stuart, in fact, was not chafing at the bit to get away to his own little nest and let his brand-new wife feather it for him. Now why would that be? I mused. I wondered if it had anything to do with my mother's cooking—or to be more precise—with his suspicions about mine. *Surely not,* I argued with myself resolutely.

I had never liked helping my mother in the kitchen. Making meals seemed such an exercise in futility. All that work and *whoosh!* It was all gone in a minute. However, it was sort of a novel idea—to have to cook now that I was married. Living in a generation that didn't question traditional roles (the man worked in the business world while the woman usually quit her job and worked in the home), I accepted the fact that the kitchen was now my sphere of responsibility, even though we had agreed that while we lived with my folks I would continue teaching. But I wanted to practice my new art in private, in my own kitchen and not on my mother's turf. My mom, seeing my dilemma, suggested I cook twice a week for the whole family. This seemed a good idea, so I set about planning my first meal.

I decided on cheese souffle and jam roly poly pudding. For a souffle to be really delicious it has to rise and be airy and light. Mine didn't! But even in its solid state it did little to fill people up.

"What's the main course?" inquired Stuart, polishing off his plate. I glared at him.

The roly poly pudding did better, except the entire family, politely savoring my handiwork, blistered their mouths with the red-hot jam.

"It's like molten lead," my new husband spluttered, diving for the water.

I was hurt. Even if it were true, I felt it quite unnecessary to mention it out loud. I noticed my dad, an extremely quiet man, grinning and thoroughly enjoying Stuart's remark. This made me madder than ever! No, I decided, the best thing would be to get away to our own little home as soon as possible in order to practice my cooking on my "victim" out of full view of the rest of the family. The problem was that my mother was an excellent cook and Stuart's mother an excellent housekeeper. The secret of good housekeeping, my mother-in-law assured me, was that everything has to have a place. I could see the sense of that, but I worried I wouldn't be able to remember which place everything had! How would our marriage survive the realization—on Stuart's part—that the days of coming home to a perfectly kept home were over, and the discovery on my part that I didn't like housekeeping very much? This disturbed me quite a bit. Somehow I had expected that having a Mrs. written on our marriage certificate would transform me into some sort of wonderful domestic genius overnight.

It would be better, I decided, when I wasn't just "helping" my mom anymore, when I stopped working and was totally responsible for everything. Then, surely, I would feel differently. Yes, I would soon learn when I had to, I told myself sternly. But I couldn't help experiencing a gnawing anxiety about whether I would really feel differently, and if I would grow to love my new "job" as much as I loved my old one. There was absolutely no question about the huge bubble of joy in my heart. I loved Stuart and loved being married—it was just that I wasn't sure I liked my homemaking role in the new partnership. Hearing our fridge had arrived and our house in Manchester was empty, I insisted we move immediately, despite the fact

I had a terrible case of bronchitis and my poor husband had to drive all the way in dense fog.

How childish of me to presume a change of location would solve things. I needed to adjust to my changed status by letting God adjust me internally. If I was supersensitive to Stuart's remarks about my souffle in Liverpool, I would be just as supersensitive if the same thing happened in Manchester. I discovered my roly poly pudding could bring out the same reaction sixty miles away (I never did learn how to get the jam cool before serving it) and trigger the identical hurt response from me. Change is an internal thing and takes time and maturity. It happens when you accept new roles and responsibilities, allowing the learning lessons to be workshops for patience, tenacity, self-control, understanding, growth, and forgiveness.

One day I decided to make a Lancashire hot pot. I knew my mother had cooked it at a very low heat, and so I did the same. I failed to realize, however, that she got it cooking first and then turned the heat down. Stuart returned from work at 6:00 P.M. tired and hungry, and inquired when dinner would be ready. I looked for the umpteenth time in the oven and realized the food had not yet started to cook. Stuart suggested we could eat something different, but I didn't have anything different. So I assured him dinner would be ready very soon. Stoically he said he didn't mind waiting a little longer and started wallpapering our bedroom. I can't remember how many times he descended the ladder to look hopefully in the direction of the stove, but at 10:00 P.M. we sat down to "raw hot pot" and in spite of the ensuing indigestion managed to laugh heartily about it all. Once you can laugh together, you'll do all right together. Laughter is not only medicine for the soul, but also builds a bridge to each other when things get tense. It's important, though, to laugh about the situation or yourself first, and not at each other!

As my husband continued to make his own adjustments to his not-very-domesticated wife, I was finding out husbandly things he wasn't very good at either. For example, he could hardly be described as a Mister-Fix-It Man. My dad was handy and pretty clever technically. He could fix things if he wanted, but chose to pay to have them seen to instead. At least they were fixed. I found that Stuart could neither fix things, nor did he choose to pay to have them done. In later years the children would even say to me, "Don't let Dad mend it. He'll only make it worse!"

When we set up our first home, however, he valiantly decided to decorate the house. He started in the bedroom and painted the ceiling white. I decided it would be prettier blue, and so without a word he climbed the ladder again and changed it. Having looked at it in daylight, I realized it didn't match the wallpaper, and so I asked him to change it back again. This time it took two coats and always looked a little gray after that—but I could see he'd had enough and wouldn't change it a third time, even for me. I was learning to read the signs—little lines that tightened round his mouth—and back off!

Next he began to hang the wallpaper. It would hang very well against the wall for a few hours but then would begin to slip slowly down till it lay in a sticky, soggy pile on the floor. After two frustrating days we hired a man to finish the job.

Our tastes in decor were evenly enough matched, though not very educated, and we chose a lovely paper (well, it looked great in the book) for our living room. We hired the same man to hang it for us. It was only when it was all finished and the workman paid and gone that we realized our mistake. It was pretty enough in the small piece in the book, but when you put it all over the walls it was quite impossible to live with. It was a bright purple with narrow white, vertical stripes, and after ten minutes or so it left your guests with a cross-eyed, glazed expression on their faces as the stripes began to move and dance. Some folk even complained about having migraine headaches after an evening with us. In fact, my brother-in-law came to visit and had to take his glasses off, saying he was sure it had given him astigmatism.

By now we began to use our mistakes as a chance to laugh and learn and not get after each other. It was important to us that we resolved these things because we did want our home to be a welcoming, pretty place. This home was not only for us, but for our friends, and the world outside our family circle that we were beginning to reach for Christ. We were ready and eager to be givers instead of takers.

I thought about the Christian homes that had opened their doors and had been such an oasis for us, and I realized we had not gone there to look at the wallpaper or sample the cooking. It was not the color of the bedroom ceiling that had drawn us there. Rather, we had gone eagerly looking for the love, laughter, and life that believers enjoy in Christ and that they would generously share with us. We had reveled in the sense of his presence in those places. I'm not saying for a minute all these houses were pigsties, but neither am I saying they were palaces. Our friends' homes reflected the gifts, personalities, and unique coupleness of each marriage. The one thing they all had in common was their love for the Lord and their love for us; that was definitely the key.

It was therefore no surprise to discover that the word *hospitality* in the Scriptures means "the love of strangers," and the commands to be hospitable are actually addressed to the elders of the assembly, and not to the little woman at home! The idea apparently was that men would warmly welcome strangers who came to worship and bring them home to wives who had varying degrees of the gift of hostessing. Now this was an exciting and liberating discovery. I worked hard to make cool roly poly puddings and souffles that rose, and Stuart made sure someone fixed whatever needed fixing. I didn't need a Ph.D. in housecraft, and Stuart didn't need to provide a mansion for his guests—we could make the best of what we had and open first our hearts and then our home to people. And so we began.

6

The First Year of Happily Ever After

Stuart

Our honeymoon was a wonderful experience. Not perfect—just wonderful. After all, I had grossly overeaten in Austria; we had grossly overexposed our lily-white British skin to the sun on the Italian Riviera; we had narrowly missed a horrendous pileup on the main express road into Brussels; we had even had an argument on the beach when I wanted Jill to play soccer and she, for some inexplicable reason, wanted only to soak up rays. But we had lived in the lap of luxury for three weeks. We had seen new sights (this was my first travel outside the British Isles), and we had reveled in the chance to be alone together—for the first time, really. In fact, I half expected to see a crowd of lively British teenagers descending on us at every turn. The problem we now had to address was, after a honeymoon like that, what do you do for an encore?

The answer was Manchester: hardly as beautiful as the Austrian Alps or as romantic as the Swiss lakes or as fascinating as the Brussels World's Fair. Just a big, old, grimy north-of-England city, famous for its role in the Industrial Revolution and battered in World War II bombing. But for the last few years of my bachelorhood it had been home.

The bank for which I worked had invited me to leave my native lake district and join the inspection staff at the head office. This was a singular honor for me, and I had moved to the big city—young, unattached, ready to enjoy my career and develop my youth ministry as opportunity presented itself. The biggest problem was finding a place to live because the bank, in paying me the honor of working on the inspection staff, didn't find it necessary to pay me very much else. The "digs" I found were really quite dreadful, the only redeeming feature being that my work required me to travel so extensively that I didn't have to be there much. My landlady was a pleasant woman, who unfortunately lived in an unpleasant home and cooked even more unpleasant food. Nearby was a YMCA hostel, where many hundreds of students and young businessmen like myself lived. I got on the waiting list, waited and waited, and one fine day I was offered a room. So I promptly packed my bags and dove into two or three of the most exciting years of my life, during which I founded an international ministry among my fellow hostel inmates, became immersed in my interesting and challenging job, and of course, met Jill.

So Manchester, grimy and bustling as it was, held and still holds a special place in my heart.

Now, of course, my landlady-dominated days were over, my all-male domicile was behind me, and my little wife and I were going to settle down in our little nest and live happily ever after. Let me tell you about the nest.

One of the most embarrassing things for a British bank in those days was having to foreclose on domestic property. One such property now owned by "my" bank was a small row of nondescript red brick houses decorously decaying in a rather pleasant but unpretentious suburb of Manchester. Needing new tenants, the bank decided to rent the houses dirt cheap to young men, newly married, whom they had moved to the big city. I applied for and was granted the privilege of renting one of these houses for the princely weekly rent of twelve shillings and six pence. It was worth a lot more than that, but it was no palace. Jill, ever the romantic, called it "gorgeous." I, the pragmatist, noticed it needed painting and fixing and wallpapering and, therefore, rated it no higher than "okay."

There was a minor problem, however, and that was my boss. For some inexplicable reason, despite his senior status, he had opted to live in this aforementioned house. And even more inexplicably, he refused to move out to let us move in. So there was nothing for Jill and me to do but wait for his exodus and in the meantime move in with the in-laws. Thankfully, they didn't seem to mind, and I thought it was great. But Jill, dreaming of her decaying red brick dream house gathering soot and grime from the Manchester fog, was longing to be there. Eventually my boss consented to leave, taking with him door handles and toilet seats and other miscellaneous items that he said were his because he'd paid for them.

Into this little nest Jill and I alighted one cold, dank, foggy day. Jill had a severe case of bronchitis, and the house was as chilly and damp as it was outdoors. Her mother and I had tried to get her to wait a day or two till she felt better and we could warm the house through for her. But she insisted on going, explaining that the new fridge was coming and she wanted to see it. We tried to point out that in her present condition it might be the last thing she ever would see, but she was adamant, so off we went from Jill's lovely, warm family home to our dark, damp dream house. The nearer we drove to Manchester, the foggier it got, the more Jill hacked and coughed, and the more we faced the reality that the honeymoon was over and happily ever after had begun.

The house didn't look too inviting from the outside and was less inviting from the inside, particularly as the furniture had not arrived. But Jill got to see her fridge, and we put a mattress on the floor, strung a blanket over the window, and packed Jill off to bed. *So this is what "better or worse" means,* I thought. Jill croaked from upstairs asking for a drink. *Ah yes,* I remembered, *"in sickness or in health."* Looking around our living room, which was tastefully furnished with a card table and two deck chairs, I thought of Jill's parents' home. *"For richer or poorer"* a little voice said, and I even caught myself thinking almost nostalgically about my old landlady and the room I rented, where the moonlight filtered softly through the holes in the drapes and projected dancing shadows of the cobwebs fastened around the solitary light bulb. *You're getting morose and morbid,* I told myself, *and you're supposed to be living happily ever after.*

I didn't exactly pull myself together. I just went to bed on the mattress with my sick little bride and tried to get warm, thinking to myself, *So this is what the wedding day was all about!* The vows and the speeches seemed far away, and the nitty-gritty business of commitment had begun— till death parted us. But as you've already realized—she survived, I survived, we survived. Not the best of starts, but at least we had made a start and moved in, and Jill had seen her new fridge.

▰▰▰▰▰▰

Many contemporary young couples, with all the modern technological aids available to them, apparently have gotten the business of having babies down to a fine art. At least that's how it sometimes appears to me. "Well, we can't start a family just yet. She needs to work while I get my degree, and then we'll both have to work for five years to pay off our school debts, etc. But then we figure we can start a family," they say.

We lived in a different age, if not on a different planet. Our approach, if I remember correctly, was "Let's do what comes naturally, and whatever comes along we'll accept as God's gift." Well, you've guessed it. A couple of months after moving to Manchester, with our little nest barely decorated, Jill dramatically fainted in a department store, and the wise older lady she was with took one look at her and said, "Jill, dear, I think you're pregnant!" When Jill told me the news, blushing appropriately, I was overjoyed momentarily before being overwhelmed totally.

Goodness, I thought, *having embarked on the most important human relationship—marriage—singularly unprepared, I am about to embark on the next most important relationship—fatherhood—even less prepared.* Jill's dad had at least given me my premarital "Don't expect anything logical" talk, but that was a lot more than any pre-parenthood preparation I had received. *Fortunately,* I thought to myself, *there are about seven months for me to get ready.* Unfortunately my work was requiring me to travel extensively. When I was home it often meant fourteen-hour workdays, leaving long and lonely stretches for Jill in a new city without much opportunity to make new friends. When I was away it was usually a Monday morning to Friday evening absence, and I had to work Saturday morning as well.

At the time, like many young husbands, I was unaware of the struggles of young wives. Jill had left her teaching profession behind in Liverpool; the lively group of young people she had led were now being led by other people;

and I was nowhere to be seen for long periods of time. But ever resourceful, she had set about being the perfect little homemaker.

■■■■■■■

In addition to my traveling for the bank I often traveled over the weekend to preach in various churches and growth groups. Before the birth of our baby Jill came with me, and we began to enjoy the first real opportunities of working together, although in those days in England the churches did not allow women to do the sort of things that God had clearly gifted Jill to do. Having had very little church experience, and having thoroughly enjoyed Cambridge Christianity among dozens of lively students and then reaching out to the youngsters in Liverpool, Jill became restive about the kind of work I was doing on weekends.

One day, on the way home from a less than earth-shaking weekend of church ministry, she said to me, "I can't believe the way you will spend time going to these dead little churches with a handful of people in them who have no intention of doing anything!" Being defensive is second nature to me, and I wasn't too happy having her criticize the "dead little churches," which were about the only kind of churches I had known all my life. So I gave her a lecture on being faithful in small things and reminded her that Jesus worked with just twelve disciples. She muttered something about him also feeding three thousand and then teaching them, but I chose to ignore that remark.

Despite my defensiveness I knew that she had a point. What's more, I was discovering something else about my wife—she had vision and drive. Never having been used to a church connected to the status quo, she was not about to learn. I knew I could not cramp her style into my hereditary style, but I also knew that for me to adopt her more reckless outreaching style created a challenge I was not overly eager to accept. So I did the masculine thing—I made some loud noises and hoped it would go away; while she did a feminine thing—she went quiet and decided to wait.

Issues can quickly become nonissues because of the advent of more significant ones. Just two months before the baby was due to arrive, my schedule required me to do an inspection of the bank managed by my friend and mentor Harry Green. My senior inspector agreed that Jill could travel with us, and although the surprise element of an inspection had to be preserved (we could not let the Greens know we were inviting ourselves to stay with them), once the surprise element was no longer important we moved in for two or three days with some of our favorite people. Jill, seven months pregnant, was ready for a change of scenery, and I was excited to have her along for the ride. Little did we guess what was in store.

Early in the morning of March 13, Friday the thirteenth as my colleagues later pointed out to me, I received a phone call.

"Stuart, this is Bernard," I heard my brother say.

"What's the matter with you?" I kidded him. "Couldn't sleep, huh?"

"Stuart, Dad's dead!"

Over thirty-five years later the chill of those words still strikes me. He was in his early fifties, and although he had struggled with angina for a few years, we were totally unprepared even to think that a coronary would whip him into eternity without warning. One minute talking to my mother, the next minute gone. I have no idea how my brother and I concluded our conversation, but I well remember going back to our room to face Jill. One look at my face and she knew without me saying a word.

"It's Pop, isn't it?" she said, and when I nodded she promptly burst into tears. She has always been freer with her emotions than me, but for the first time in years I cried, too. We held each other, saying nothing, only knowing deep down that when two are one, even the grief of one becomes the grief of both. She sorrowed for herself at one level, even though she and my dad had enjoyed far too few opportunities to be together. She sorrowed for my sorrow much more.

On the ride to my mother's home I discovered Jill's sensitivities had depths I had never dreamed of. Of course, we were having another lesson in marriage—the lesson that marriage is the adjustment of two people as together they embrace the changing scenes of life. We had adjusted to Manchester vis-à-vis Liverpool, our house vis-à-vis Jill's home, being together rather than being separate. But we were discovering that marriage is a relationship where two people are instinctively available to each other at the point of need or the moment of opportunity.

There is a kind of emotional numbness associated with dramatic trauma. My mother, my brother, and I all experienced it after the news of Pop's death, and we recognized it as one of God's gracious provisions to help human beings cope with the shocking circumstances of life. But the numbness can also produce an inertia. My mother's first words on our arrival were, "What are we going to do?" The moment she said these words I realized the unpleasant truth that I had suddenly been thrust into the position of head of the family in my mother's eyes. Frankly, the only answer I knew was, "I don't know"—and I didn't.

But Jill had another surprise. She, without any previous experience of bereavement, seemed to sense what was necessary. Even though she had only joined the family a few months earlier I noted a quiet calmness about her demeanor. She took charge as she went about doing a host of small but necessary things to keep the family functioning and to get us through the early hours of grief. I was getting to know the woman I had married, and the subsequent years have confirmed what she showed that sad day. When the chips are down and when push comes to shove, she has reserves of strength and resolve that only traumatic, challenging situations bring to light.

Only a few weeks after my father's death we experienced another crisis of an entirely different kind. Death gave way to life. One generation passed on, and another took center stage. Our firstborn, David, decided it was time to be born. Jill's mother, ever overprotective, had prevailed upon us to move back to Liverpool a few weeks before the due date so that Jill would get "proper care"—as opposed, presumably, to the "improper care" she suggested would be meted out in Manchester. So we went.

Early on the morning of May 22, 1959 I was awakened from my well-deserved rest by a strange feeling that two holes were being bored into my head. Sitting up with a start I saw Jill squatting on the bed, looking at me with a piercing intensity that was matched by her words when she said, "Stu, the baby's coming." For some unknown reason, without a moment's hesitation I said, "Don't be silly. Go back to sleep. It's only six o'clock." Thirty-five years later my blood curdles at the thought! I don't know what Jill did, but in the interest of strict honesty I must confess that I rolled over and went back to sleep.

Later that morning I was urged by the combined forces of my wife and mother-in-law to take Jill to the hospital. A strange sensation of total irrelevance began to overwhelm me as I realized that Jill was on her own now, that she was turning to her mother, who was considerably more experienced than me in the art of giving birth. The people bustling around Jill were all female and seemed to be thoroughly competent. So I did what men used to do in those far-off days: I jumped in my car and went to work fifty miles away. Jill worked hard all that day and the following night. I checked in, was firmly and courteously shunted out of the way, decided there was nothing I could do, so I went to work the next day—a Saturday. Round about noon, as I was miles away, our first little boy entered the world. As I calculated how long it was since Jill had told me, "The baby's coming"—thirty hours to be exact—I congratulated myself that I had been right in questioning whether this was the time or not. But because discretion is the better part of valor I, of course, said nothing!

I'm sure that modern parents are horrified at this account of what happened when babies were born in England in the Middle Ages—or the fifties and sixties—but that's how it was in those days. Different times, different places, different cultures, but one thing has not changed—the inevitable, inexplicable joy of becoming parents and together realizing that two failing people have combined, under God, to make a person and have now been commissioned by God to raise the child to be fit for earth and ready for eternity.

　　　　　　　　　　　　　　＊＊＊＊＊＊

There was a new look in Jill's eyes when I walked into her hospital room. She was in bed holding her tiny bundle of eternal boy. I wouldn't call the look inscrutable, but it was mysterious, strangely knowing. The look of a woman introduced to that which man can never know, a look that mutely said, *I have given birth; I have gazed as near to the core of the mystery of life as humans can go.* My little wife was a mother! I made sure she was okay, hugged her tenderly, not knowing if she would break, and then looked at my boy. He looked slightly the worse for wear, but I suspected that he was in much better shape than I had been at the same stage in my career.

My mother told me one day that after I had been introduced to this world with the aid of forceps, she had taken one look at my misshapen head, burst into tears, and said, "Oh, I didn't want a baby that looked like that!" I suspect that some of my detractors, on hearing that confession, will nod their heads wisely and say, "We suspected that he had been subjected to some deep emotional trauma at a very early stage in his development. That explains a lot!"

I have no idea what preborns and newborns hear or sense, but our little guy could only have heard *oohs* and *aahs* and felt warm, welcoming embraces.

Jill said, "Take him—he's your son!"

I had the strangest feeling of being on the edge of panic. "How hard do I hold him?" "What if I drop him?" and irrationally, "What will he think of me?"

I did take him, gingerly. He opened one eye halfway, gave me a suspicious look, and promptly shut his eye firmly. "I don't think he's impressed." I laughed with just a tinge of apprehension.

"Don't worry," said Jill. "He'll soon get used to you. The nurse has called him Sean," she volunteered. "She's Irish, you see."

"Sean!" I replied. "You want to call him Sean?"

"No, dear," she laughed. "I don't; the nurse does. In fact, look in the baby's crib." I did, and sure enough, there was a neat little label with "Sean Briscoe" in plain letters.

"His name is David," I insisted, feeling vaguely like John the Baptist's dad announcing, "His name is John."

"I know, honey," Jill replied. "Calm down. He's David after your grandfather David Henry Wardle and after you, David Stuart Briscoe, and I think we should add Stanley in honor of your dad who never saw a grandchild."

"That makes two David S. Briscoes," I commented.

"All right, let's add Campbell after our favorite evangelist Campbell McAlpine," Jill suggested.

"David Stanley Campbell Briscoe seems an awfully long name for such a little fellow!" I said.

"He'll grow into it, just you see. His name is a statement of his heritage—a daily reminder of his special roots."

"Right, and it says something about our hopes and aspirations for him," I agreed.

We looked again at our little boy with the long name, and instinctively Jill and I bowed our heads and lifted our hearts. Words of thanksgiving tumbled forth, confessions of unworthiness followed, and heartfelt cries for wisdom and grace and everything else necessary soared to the throne above. The little boy who had been thoroughly prayed for in the womb slept peacefully now, breathing in the fresh air of a prayer-filled room. His first hours on earth were already touched with the fragrance of heaven.

An officious nurse, as stiff in manner as she was starched in uniform, informed me in no uncertain terms that my time was up. So I dutifully bade my little family farewell, feeling again that slight tinge of irrelevance, and drove home to meet my mother-in-law, whom we had made into a brand-new grandmother without even asking her permission.

I think I must have had my feet firmly planted in midair because I suddenly noticed the startled look on a policeman's face as I began to overtake him at a speed far exceeding the speed limit. Perhaps he was so startled he forgot his duty, or maybe he could see "new dad" written all over my face. I'll never know, but he took no action and I breathed again.

Was that a heavenly chuckle I heard? I think so, and it was accompanied with the most overwhelming sense of God's goodness to me. The first year of living happily ever after was not quite complete, but it had been full.

7

And Baby Makes Free

$\mathcal{J}$ had just discovered I was pregnant. But becoming pregnant was one thing; having a baby was quite another! As Stuart has said, we hadn't really discussed when to start our family. Living in a generation when, to get married was to get kids, we fully expected to produce children whenever it happened to happen.

We were thrilled. Now we really would have a home in every sense of the word. It never crossed our minds to withdraw from ministry because of our babies. Rather, the arrival of our children gave us a great sense of anticipation and excitement as we realized our little family could be the means of help and blessing to other families. We weren't quite sure how we would work it all out, but hadn't we both come to share the verse that said, "As for me and my house *we* will serve the Lord"? Well, now the first "we" was about to make his appearance!

We accumulated the mountain of paraphernalia that accompanies such an event, shared our exciting news with our family and friends, and resolved to become the best parents we could possibly be. Sitting in our living room with my eyes shut (the wallpaper that made you dizzy was still firmly in place, since Stuart hadn't hung it!), I realized the baby was about due. I opened my eyes and looked at my husband. He was sitting opposite me, absorbed with the business news. The paper hid his face, and my eyes fastened on the black print of the newspaper as I wondered what was happening in the big bad world "out there." In here it was warm and cozy, safe and secure. But we were about to introduce a little eternal person into the equation.

Suddenly the huge implications of this momentous event totally overwhelmed me. Panic began in my shoes, moved rapidly to my heart, and found its expression in anxious tears. I began to weep, quietly, so I wouldn't disturb my beloved. However, I'm not very good at weeping quietly, and my concerned spouse, hearing the sound of my sorrow, lowered his newspaper and asked, "Whatever is the matter, Jill?"

What was the matter? I wondered. How could I explain this sense of total panic? How could Stuart understand anyway, since he was a man?

Then another emotion caught me off guard and I burst out, "I want my mother!"

"What for?" Stuart inquired with kindly surprise.

I couldn't answer him. How could I say, "Because she knows what I feel like, having been where I am—twice. Because she's a woman and understands; she knows the intensity of this fear that comes with the realization that this baby is going to be born and nothing in the heavens above or the earth below will stop it happening." Why did I suddenly and overwhelmingly want my mother? I asked myself. Because I couldn't have her perhaps, or because that part of my life was over? I knew I was supposed to have transferred my dependence to my new love and partner, and I had—totally, gladly, and with abandon!

Yet in that moment I inexplicably needed my mother. I needed to hear her say, "It will be all right, Jill. You can do it because you were created to do it. Birth is the most natural thing in the world. It will surely happen, and after a short day or two you will forget the shock of the pain in the joy that a child has been born. You'll see."

My husband eyed me with real concern and added his typically manly and pragmatic comment to my thinking, "Just think of every person on earth. Each one constitutes a birth!" He smiled with satisfaction and returned to the stock market. He was right of course—it was just hard to let such logical thinking harness my panic and ride it to a standstill.

Shortly afterward we packed our bags and traveled to Liverpool, where we had decided the baby would be born. So God gave me my mother after all, and, armed with such moral support from two of the people closest to me, I was ready to see our child "constitute one more birth."

Two days later, pretty much on schedule, I woke in the early hours of the morning knowing our baby had begun its long journey into our arms. Sitting up in bed, I looked at Stuart, who was sleeping the sleep of the just. How could he sleep so soundly! I asked myself indignantly, watching him slumbering happily on. I glared at him. If he didn't know what was happening to me, he should! I thought fiercely. Yes, he should wake up automatically like I had done and just "know" that this was it. Stuart's snores continued unaffected until, in his own words, he became aware, somnolent as he was, of two piercing gray eyes probing him into consciousness. As soon as I saw a glimmer of recognition, I announced emphatically, "The baby's coming." He smiled and said gently but firmly, "Nonsense, go back to sleep"—and promptly did. I couldn't believe it!

But sure enough he was nearly right, as the birth process had indeed only just begun. It was a full thirty hours later that our firstborn son announced his glad arrival, and I swear all the angels of heaven clapped their hands. We were parents and we glorified God, held each other close, and gazed at our precious child, saying in our hearts, *Look out world, here we come!*

Back at my mother's for a few days, Stuart and I adjusted to a no-sleep routine and were introduced to the fact that having a newborn means waking up to the selfishness in one's character.

"I never realized how utterly selfish I have been all my life," I commented to my mother.

"I tried to tell you, Jill," my mom teased, although both of us knew there was more than a little truth in her quip.

"When a newborn cries it doesn't matter how tuckered out you are, it's time to jump," I observed. "Someone should market newborns as 'de-selfishing' agents."

I found myself totally absorbed twenty-four hours a day with the baby. Back in Manchester, even with the wonderful help of my mom-in-law, who came for a few days, my world revolved around David. "And rightly so," Stuart's mom said with great emphasis. "That's how God intends it to be!" I had no argument with her statement. As I have already mentioned, we were living in a role-oriented generation, where the married woman's place was in the home and the man's in the marketplace, and I was happy to relinquish my career for—in my eyes—a higher calling. It wasn't the career issue that I faced, but the ministry issue. Did the baby make three—or free?

"Free," Stuart affirmed with great emphasis. "Having our baby has given you a greater freedom. You're not tied to a nine-to-five job now. You are master of your own schedule."

"But my schedule is totally full of baby," I pointed out. "Some would even call that bondage." As we discussed it, I realized there was indeed a freedom within my marvelous new responsibility. I was free to use my mothering day to meet and influence a whole new world of mothers David had introduced me to. God opened my eyes to the young marrieds who lived in our cul-de-sac, the young moms I met during my visits to the clinic, and those like me who wrestled with their babies at the long supermarket lines.

How had I missed this world of mothers? I marveled. *Perhaps,* I ruminated, *it takes a young mother to see a young mother.* And then there was the park. An English mom living in the fifties would take her young charges to the pretty parks, sit on a bench, and while her little ones sat in the lovely, high, big-wheeled prams or played on the swings, would chatter away to others just like her.

Suddenly I became very excited. I saw our common interest as a bridge and realized I could use this mothering season to introduce my new friends to the Lord. I didn't need to wait until our children left for college to have a ministry. My mission field was between my own two feet, and indeed Stuart was right that "baby made free." It would have been so easy for me to use David as an excuse to opt out of ministry. Instead our baby became a happy part of the calling we had accepted as a family.

Having a baby so soon after getting married gave us another emotional workshop. We had hardly had a chance to adjust to the idea of being Mr. and Mrs. before we also became Mom and Dad. To take on so many new roles all at once was a challenge, not least in the area of our devotional lives.

Our very different temperaments affected the way we read the Word of God and prayed together. My devotional habits were deeply influenced by a friend who had introduced me to the importance of having a personal time with God every day. Right from the start of my Christian life I realized a relationship with God could never survive unless we talked together regularly. Any relationship has to grow through communication, and it made absolute sense to me that I needed to talk to God about the things he was saying to me as I began to read his Word.

I adopted a simple plan whereby I read a portion of Scripture, followed it with a prayer response, then recorded my thoughts from this exercise in a devotional diary. I also kept lists of people's needs and learned to pray diligently for these. Imagine my delight to find those specific prayer requests answered! It was almost like having a wish list come true every time I made one. At first I was tempted to wonder if it was a matter of happenstance, but as I set about taking other people's problems as well as my own to my heavenly Father, earnestly asking for answers and solutions, I discovered a whole new world of possibilities. Prayer really did make a difference.

What's more, I could get on my knees and "travel" the world in a split second, arriving in Africa, India, or the Far East as soon as I began to pray. I could talk to my heavenly Father about specific missionaries, their children, or their work. I could actually help. From halfway around the world I could be a part of the purposes of God.

A friend told me about a missionary traveling through a dangerous place. Robbers were waiting to steal the church funds he was carrying, but they saw four soldiers guarding the missionary, so they didn't attack him as they had planned. When the robbers told their story in the village through which the missionary passed, they were told there were no soldiers with the man of God. But there were four little old ladies in a drawing room in the south of England who were on their knees praying for him—at that exact time. I was thrilled. I had no reason to doubt the story. I could be a prayer soldier too!

And so as a young believer I began to thoroughly discipline myself routinely to keep informed and pray about Christian work overseas, but also to study the Scriptures, apply them to my life, and pray about the personal implications. All this devotional activity had hitherto taken place precisely between seven and eight every morning—until the baby came.

Even after our marriage I had kept up these disciplined and somewhat rigid habits, using other times of the day to pray with my husband. But one can't do much praying or meditating when one's baby is screaming, which invariably happened as soon as I dared to put him down and pick up my Bible. And it always seemed he was hungry that same hour each morning.

"Stuart," I moaned, "you know I've had my golden rule severely tested."

"You mean your 'no Bible, no breakfast' rule?" my husband inquired.

"It's worked like a dream up to now," I replied, nodding in the affirmative. "But David doesn't seem to understand, and the dream is turning into a nightmare."

"Why don't you have your devotions after he's asleep?" said Stuart, suggesting the obvious. But the obvious isn't always acceptable, and I struggled with the challenge of a change in an area of my life that had almost become a sacred cow.

Shouldn't the baby fit into our schedule? I wondered. But David continued to be a typical newborn, and I realized I had to change. And so my strict, inflexible schedule began to bend.

Then another problem surfaced. Stuart and I were finding our individual methods of devotional exercises so different they actually began to be a bone of contention between us.

It wasn't that we were arguing over having devotions (Stuart's rule of life has always been "Never put your head on the pillow until you've had your nose in the Book"). Rather the timing and method of such endeavors became a flashpoint.

To begin with, we found our emphasis was different. I spent most of my devotional time in prayer, which I thoroughly enjoyed, while Stuart spent nearly all of his time in the Scriptures, which he thoroughly enjoyed. "After all," he said in his typically logical fashion, "it's obviously a lot more important to let God talk to us than for us to talk to him."

That did indeed seem perfectly logical, but being somewhat more mystical in nature, I felt my prayer life was a whole lot more than just talking. "I worship," I announced triumphantly. Whereupon Stuart carefully explained the meaning of worship with a thorough exposition of the word!

However are we going to get our devotional lives together? I wondered. *And do we need to? When will we find time to do so? And if this is what it's like with one baby, should we ever have another?* If I didn't have my quiet time first thing in the morning, I began to look fearfully heavenward, convinced the sky was about to fall on my head in judgment. My favorite chorus was:

> In the morning first of all,
> Savior, let me hear Thy call.
> Make me ready to obey
> Thy commands throughout the day.

So what would happen if I couldn't read my Bible and pray "first of all"? How could I hear his commands throughout the day if he and I hadn't met early in the morning? Stuart cheerfully pointed out we could talk to our Father anywhere, anytime. It was a question of just being flexible enough to snatch the unexpected space that might open up in our waking hours, he explained. I panicked. I couldn't pray "on the run," and I didn't think that was very reverent anyway. Why couldn't Stuart see it was obviously a lot better to do it my way?

As we tried to put all this together with the added intrusion of our newborn, another element entered in. When we actually did manage to have a time together with God, it usually ended up in disaster. Knowing my husband's style of study, my eye would run down the passage we read together and I would think to myself, *I know exactly what he's going to say about this. It will be precise, ordered, tidily under three headings, and all the headings will begin with the same letter.*

Meanwhile my husband was thinking, *I know exactly what Jill will do with this. She'll have a great time "peeking around the corner of the verse" as she says, seeing all sorts of things that aren't even there, and allegorizing it all.* We would begin to share our findings, find out our suspicions had been correct, and end up arguing about it. I was discouraged; Stuart was not. He simply said, "This isn't going to work. Instead let's share one thought from our own study that is meaningful to each of us and then pray."

But I couldn't leave it alone. How could a Christian couple argue about their devotional time? What was wrong with my husband, or was it me? "There's nothing wrong with either of us," Stuart insisted. "We just approach this in totally different ways. Neither way is wrong—just different. So let's continue to have our own individual devotional times and major on prayer."

And so that is what we began to do. We read individually, shared a special thought (I entered both in my diary), and then we would pray. We also selected a good missionary biography (the first was the life of Hudson Taylor) and read a chapter a night. We couldn't argue about that!

I slowly acclimated to my husband's suggestion of using the unexpected moment, giving up my rigidity with difficulty, but forced by my baby's needs to do so—and that was good for me. Stuart meanwhile gave himself to learning to enjoy prayer as much as I did. It worked. I learned to pray on the run and saw to my great surprise just as many prayers answered as when I used to pray at 7:20 every morning. Stuart learned to listen to my bright-eyed discoveries as I peeked happily and busily around the corners of verses.

"Do you think Mrs. Noah liked animals?" I chattered excitedly one day. Stuart managed to give it some thought. He resisted the temptation to dismiss the triviality of my question, and I was able to tell him it had made me wonder if she found her tasks easy or hard, and if God wanted us to be obedient whether we "liked" what we had to do or not. He learned I did have a reason for my wild wonderings. And I learned some basic rules of interpreting the Scriptures and the difference between eisegesis and exegesis, which, being interpreted, is the difference between reading into the text what you wish were there, and getting out of the text what was intended to be there.

One thing, however, Stuart has always managed to do for me is to point out the "principle" of the Scripture. I always wanted to rush on to the practical application without understanding the content or context of it. I began to watch a man who loved God's Word so deeply and avidly he could always be found under piles of books somewhere. They would not perhaps be near the bookshelf because he was seldom in the course of his busy day near a bookshelf. The books would be near him. If he was washing the car, there would be one open on a rain barrel nearby. When he made some phone calls, I'd see two or three borrowed volumes being fingered longingly, as if he were anxious to be done with tasks in order to return to the supreme task—that of figuring out God's Word and purposes, grasping a little of the supreme scope of God's thoughts.

I loved him for his zeal and his drive to learn. He insisted on knowing and thinking, reaching and stretching, digging, yea, excavating. I found him looking under every inflection of Scripture, fully expecting to find hidden treasure all day long. This didn't mean the practical tasks were neglected; it just meant the two were inseparable. The spiritual was practical—the practical, spiritual. Work was worship; worship was work!

"You'll never grow old," I told him. "People who are never done with wanting to know don't, you know."

"Jill, there's so much I want to know," he said very quietly and seriously. "So much I need to learn about everything!" It's funny—thirty-five years later he's still saying those very same words—practically every day. But then that's what happens when you never put your head on the pillow if you haven't had your nose in the Book. I decided to swap my rule—"No Bible, no breakfast"—for his.

One day as my baby slept in my arms so my nose could be in the Book I read Acts 1:8:

> But you will receive power when the Holy Spirit comes on you; and you will be my witnesses in Jerusalem, and in all Judea and Samaria, and to the ends of the earth.

I lifted up my eyes and looked out the window. It was a gray day—nothing new. The gaudy sign hanging above the "Cat's Whisker," a teenage hangout, bent with the breeze. Could "beginning at Jerusalem" mean "Get yourself over the road into that place and tell them about Jesus"? Somehow I knew that's exactly what it did mean for me. "What do you think, David?" I whispered to my sleeping child. He smiled.

8

Loosened around the Edges

Stuart

Do you remember the conversation Jill and I had concerning the "dead little churches"? I didn't appreciate Jill's less-than-enthusiastic interest in them, compared with her exuberant interest in the kids outside the church. Well, as I told you, I hoped the subject would go away, but Jill waited for it to return. It did.

Across the street from our little home was a coffee bar called the "Cat's Whisker." In those days British young people liked to congregate in this sort of place where they could listen to their music—it was the era of the Beatles— meet their friends, drink coffee, and grow their hair. Most of the coffee bars were noisy and crowded and more or less harmless. They served to keep the kids off the street and out of trouble most of the time. Some of them, as we would see later, were absolute dens of iniquity. The "Cat's Whisker" was not one of them.

One day as I was looking out of the window at the crowds of teenagers milling around the "Cat's Whisker" I was thinking to myself, *We really should be doing something about those kids. Jill's right!* But I'm afraid I didn't want to admit she was right, and I certainly didn't want to admit

I was apprehensive. *It's strange,* I thought. *I wasn't scared when I played rugby, and I wasn't unduly perturbed in my Royal Marine days. And it doesn't bother me at all to get up in front of a crowd and speak to them. But I don't want to go over there!*

Jill, having decided that her big, brave husband was not going to do anything, had been quietly training three or four young people from the church we were attending to take a survey that was designed to open up a conversation on spiritual matters. She then told them to go over to the "Cat's Whisker" and see if the kids would respond. I might add that she apparently was having second thoughts about going, too. She had told them, "I must stay and look after the baby, but I'll be praying!" She admitted later that she had been having a fit of the "here am I, send them" syndrome.

The youngsters dutifully did as they were told, fearing the worst. But, as is so often the case, the worst never happened. As they arrived at the door of the coffee bar, all the kids, dozens of them, spilled out onto the sidewalk because the owner had kicked them all out for unruly behavior. With nothing to do and all night to do it, the kids were standing around when one of the young survey-takers volunteered, "Why don't you come over to the house where the lady is peeping through the curtains? She'll give you some coffee, and you can get inside out of the cold."

And so off they marched to be greeted by a nonplussed Jill and her firstborn son. The kids filled every room of the house, waiting for the coffee, which Jill began to make as quickly as possible. When all the coffee had been consumed Jill stood in the hallway and told them her story and the stories of her kids in Liverpool. The "Cat's Whisker" kids listened intently. Never having been to church and never having had the church come to them, they were hearing something totally new and strange. It was interesting and puzzling to them.

Just as Jill was running out of things to say I arrived home after a long journey from the small church where I had been preaching. At least I tried to arrive home, but as I pushed my front door it stuck. I pushed harder, and to my surprise a strange-looking young person with long hair dyed in a variety of colors stuck his (or her, I couldn't tell) head around the door and said, "Hey, go easy, Who're ya pushing? Can't you see we're full up!" I found myself in the unaccustomed situation of pleading with a total stranger to let me into my own house. Fortunately, Jill realized what was happening and prevailed upon the young man to grant me access.

"What in the world is going on?" I asked Jill, looking up the stairs and down the hallway at wall-to-wall teenagers.

"I can explain everything," she responded hurriedly, "but first just talk to them."

"What am I supposed to tell them? I don't even know who they are."

"Tell them what you told the people in church tonight," she suggested.

So I embarked on a greatly abbreviated and simplified version of my sermon. Watching the reactions of the young people carefully I could hardly believe their interest and attention. Eventually we made arrangements to have them come back, they invited us to visit the "Cat's Whisker," and they went home. That night after we had restored our home to some semblance of order we fell into bed tired and elated.

"Some day of rest this has been!" I said, reflecting on my Sunday and thinking of Monday only a few hours away.

"I know, honey," said Jill, "but you wouldn't want it any other way, would you?"

"No," I answered quite truthfully.

"When should we go across to the 'Cat's Whisker'?" she asked with characteristic enthusiasm.

"Not tonight," I replied with characteristic lack of enthusiasm. "I'm going to sleep. Monday's nearly here, and they pay me to be at least half awake, you know, and the baby will be awake in an hour." But tired as we were, we didn't sleep because we sensed God had opened a door of opportunity for us that would lead to an entirely new life.

▰▰▰▰▰▰

One night, soon after the events of that famous Sunday, I ventured into the "Cat's Whisker," dressed as casually as a young bank inspector's wardrobe would allow. I looked as conspicuous as a petunia in an onion patch.

"What do ya want?" asked a rough-looking young man.

"Oh, I just came in to talk," I replied.

"Okay, talk to me and my chick," he suggested, pointing to his "chick," who turned out to be a slim, pale-faced girl clad in leather and chains and a liberal application of mascara.

Taken aback by his openness, I blurted out, "All right. Are you—er—are you alive?"

He looked a little startled (so did I, for that matter) but answered, "Of course I'm alive."

"Why?" I asked.

"Why does there have to be a 'why'?" he retorted.

Warming to the discussion, I said, "Can you see anything in this room that does not have a purpose? The table, the chair, the coffee cup, the guitar?"

"No."

"Are they greater or lesser than you?" I inquired.

"Lesser, of course."

"Then if you are greater than things you admit have a purpose, isn't it reasonable to assume you have a purpose?"

"Yes, I suppose it is. But I've never thought about it." He paused for a moment and then added with a grin, "I've just thought of something. I know why I'm alive."

"Tell me," I said quickly.

"I'm alive because I was born and haven't died," he announced triumphantly.

"Fantastic," said his girlfriend. "Did you think that up all by yourself?"

"Let me ask you something," I said quietly after I acknowledged he had made a good point. "Did you have anything to do with your birth?"

"No. Except I was there."

"Do you plan to have anything to do with your death?" I pressed on.

"No, I certainly don't," he responded seriously.

"Then as far as you're concerned you are alive because an accident outside your control brought you into being and you're waiting till another accident takes you out," I suggested.

He thought for a moment and then said with utter sincerity, "You know something, I'm an accident suspended between accidents."

We sat quietly for a while, and then I said, "I've got news for you."

"Tell me," he urged, learning forward on his elbows.

"You're no accident. You were created. You are significant. You are . . . " and I launched into an explanation of the good news of God's plan for mankind, including him and his "chick." He listened with total concentration, oblivious to the noise and the crowd. When I had finished I asked him, "Do you believe that?"

"No," he replied promptly. "And neither do you."

I was totally shocked. "What d'you mean? Of course I believe it," I remonstrated.

"No, you don't, and I'll tell you how I know you don't. This story is so wonderful that if you really believed it you would have been down here before tonight to tell us," he almost shouted at me. Then after getting up he walked away, looking over his shoulder long enough to say, "It was nice talking to you. Good night."

Jill was waiting for me when I got home, eager to hear what had happened. I could hardly tell her what had transpired because I was so stung and unnerved by what the young man had said. I knew I believed the gospel with all my heart, but I was discovering I believed it for myself but did not really believe it for anyone else. Oh sure, I preached to the people in church, but I knew and they knew I was basically trying to convert the converted and convince the convinced.

As Jill and I talked long into the night we sensed a strange stirring in our hearts. We had always been open to the possibility of being involved in career ministry but had taken the passive route, determining that we would not actively seek out opportunities for being involved in ministry at the expense of being fully involved laypeople in the marketplace. In fact, we had promised the Lord that if he wanted me out of the bank we would go without hesitation, but the initiative would have to come from the outside and not from us. Jill has a theory that when God wants to lead you into a new situation he loosens you around the edges in much the same way that you get a pie out of a dish. We were being loosened around the edges!

━━━━━━

When she was still at Cambridge Jill had met a particularly charming and energetic lady called Molly MacKenzie. Mrs. MacKenzie belonged to an organization called Pocket Testament League, which, as its name suggested, had been formed to distribute copies of the New Testament or parts thereof to people around the world who did not possess them. The work had developed into a lively, effective ministry reaching people in all walks of life.

Now, in the midst of having our eyes opened to the possibility of full-time ministry, Mrs. MacKenzie came to stay with us overnight. We talked about the "Cat's Whisker." Her eyes gleamed. We wondered aloud to her if God was telling us he had a change in mind for us. To our utter incredulity she said, "Oh, yes. I think he wants you full time with Pocket Testament League." We talked a little more. She went happily off to bed, and we went soberly to another sleepless night. We had no idea where to go from there, but we prayed and asked the Lord to deliver us from making a mistake. Then we heard from Mrs. MacKenzie that the chairman of Pocket Testament League would like to travel up to see us. Things were moving a little too quickly for me and nowhere quickly enough for Jill.

I was learning that when steps of faith need to be taken, Jill's attitude tends to be, "You pray, honey. I'll pack."

"Jill, we must be careful not to make an emotional decision," I insisted.

"But how exactly are we going to make a decision? I realize you're looking at giving up a career. I've already given up mine, but I suppose I could always teach again," she agreed.

"I don't think I'll be reluctant to walk away from the bank if I'm sure I should. I'm not afraid of losing a career so much as making a false turn," I explained.

"Then let's ask God to do something specific when we meet Mr. Anderson, the chairman."

"Like what?" I asked dubiously. "You're not putting out a fleece, are you?"

"Well, Gideon did, and God didn't seem to mind."

"But how d'you know the difference between a fleece and a coincidence?" I asked.

91

"You don't, unless you have asked God graciously to work even through a coincidence."

"All right," I said, not altogether convinced. "What should we ask him to do?"

"Well, we can ask him to meet our needs, and we need a house, so let's say if Mr. Anderson tells us how they plan to meet our housing needs then we'll quit the bank and go with Pocket Testament League."

"Are you sure?" I asked. Then, seeing the excited look on her face, I added, "I can see you are. Okay, let's do it!"

❦❦❦❦❦❦

But then something else unexpected happened. Our dear friend Mr. L.A.T. Van Dooren, the principal of Capernwray Bible School, called on the phone and said, "Stuart, Major Thomas wants to talk to you on Saturday morning at eight o'clock in London. He's coming in from Germany and leaving immediately for New Zealand."

"What does he want?" I asked, wondering how I could possibly get from Manchester to London and back between finishing work on Friday night and being home in time for Mr. Anderson Saturday evening.

"He wants to ask you if you'd be interested in coming to work with us as secretary of the Capernwray Missionary Fellowship of Torchbearers," he replied. I felt weak.

"I'll make it somehow, Van," I replied and hung up.

"What was that all about?" Jill inquired. I told her, admittedly with a tremor in my voice, hardly daring to believe what was happening to us.

"It's one thing to ask the Lord to send someone to us if he wants us in the ministry," I said ruefully, "but two in one week is too much!"

"I don't know about too much," Jill replied. "But he's certainly loosening us around the edges."

××××××

We had no sooner gotten used to the idea of looking at two opportunities when the chief inspector with whom I was working called me into his office. "I've got great news for you, young man," he said. "Your time on the inspection staff is complete, and I've recommended you to the general managers, and they want to meet you on Monday. They'll probably offer you a position on their staff."

This was my professional dream come true. Suddenly Pocket Testament League and Capernwray Missionary Fellowship and "Cat's Whisker" and all those kids slipped into the background and the banking fast-track was opening up before me. "Oh, thank you, sir," I gushed. "That's wonderful."

"Guess what!" I burst out to Jill as I rushed into the house that evening, spilling out my excitement about the bank interview.

"But what about the way God has been leading us?" she asked.

"Well maybe he's leading me to stay in the bank. He needs people in the business world, you know."

"I know all that. But we did promise we would go if he issued a call to us, and he's sent two in a week."

"Maybe he sent three," I replied, trying to sound convincing. Then suddenly I thought, *It's okay. I see Major Thomas on Saturday morning, Mr. Anderson on Saturday night, and the general managers on Monday. That will give me time to see what the ministries are saying before I meet the bank people. I need to do it that way because if the bank*

even suspects I might be considering leaving that will be the
kiss of death to my possible promotion.

Jill said nothing, but I knew she was as troubled as I was
torn. On Friday afternoon, a few short hours before I was
to travel overnight to London, I received a phone call from
the general manager's office.

"Mr. Briscoe, the general managers want to see you in
half an hour."

I had been working all day in the vaults of a large branch,
checking deeds, some of which had been accumulating dust
for years. I rushed to the men's room to try and wash off
most of the grime and made a hurried call to Jill, who said
with ill-disguised anxiety in her voice, "What are you going
to say to them?"

"I've no idea, but as little as possible. I have to keep all
my options open." Then with minutes to spare I prayed,
"Lord, don't let me make a mistake."

Opening my New Testament where I had finished reading that morning I read words that burned into my soul:
"Lift up your eyes and look on the fields. They are white
already to harvest." I closed my Testament, uttered a
"Thank you, Lord," and, taking a deep breath, went for my
interview. Ushered into a plush office that I had never seen
before, I was introduced to the three general managers, all
of whom I had never seen before.

"Please be seated, Mr. Briscoe," said the chairman. "We
have followed your career with great interest, young man.
Now tell us, what exactly are your ambitions?"

I knew the answer they wanted and expected: "Sir, my
ambition is to serve the bank as well as I possibly can, to
the best of my abilities, wherever you feel I can be of most
use to the company." I knew the words, but they wouldn't
come out. *"Lift up your eyes,"* said a little voice. Jill's
troubled look came to mind.

"My ambitions, sir?" I replied. "I think I have a surprise for you. My ambition is to serve the Lord Jesus, probably in the ministry. In fact, I have two interviews this weekend with people who have invited me to work with them." I should point out that the year was 1959, the place was the general managers' office in a British bank, where the rule of thumb was you commit yourself for life to the bank and the bank will commit itself to you "till death do us part." In those days, once you were in the bank nobody left unless he was shown the door.

There was a stunned silence. The general managers looked at each other, and I suddenly realized my career was down the tubes and it didn't matter. The next half hour was spent explaining why I was going to do what I was going to do. What I meant by evangelism. Why I thought it necessary to talk to people about such a personal subject as religion. Was there a possibility I might be ever so slightly carried away? one of the general managers asked.

Strangely, I felt perfectly relaxed, thoroughly enjoying myself, and so privileged to be able to talk to those three gracious, respected men about my faith. At last one of them looked at his watch and said with a smile, "Well, Mr. Briscoe, d'you think we could talk banking for a few minutes? We seem to have covered religion pretty thoroughly." We did, and I left the room.

The chief inspector, a great man whom I deeply respected, had waited for me. "How did it go?" he asked.

"I've announced I'm leaving the bank and going into the ministry."

He sat down with a thump, put his hand on his chest, and said, "You young rascal, don't give me shocks like that!"

"I'm sorry I gave you a shock, sir," I replied. "But I'm serious."

The room was totally silent. Then quietly he said, "I don't know your God the way you do, but I want you to know that he won't let you down, and if you find you made a mistake, come back, and I'll get you back on track." Then he added with a gentle smile, "I don't think you'll be back."

To the best of my recollection that was the only really emotional moment for me in that staid, correct, formal, and wonderful bank. I wanted to hug him, but as we were British we shook hands. I think there was a tear in his eye. There were some in mine.

That night I booked a sleeping compartment on the Manchester-to-London train, but I think I wasted my money. My mind was in a whirl. Jill had been delighted when I told her about the interview. She was already ready to go—I was rapidly getting there. But it was one thing to be ready to go—it was another thing to know where.

I had known Major Ian Thomas and his ministry to European young people for a number of years, although we had spent very little time together. He was extremely busy rushing around the world, and I was usually one in a crowd whenever I was close to him. I was, therefore, looking forward to some time with him and quite interested in knowing why he was interested in my joining him in his ministry. He had never heard me preach, although I had heard him many times. Indeed, I had been greatly helped through his characteristically vigorous preaching that concentrated on the fact that the Christ who died for us to save us from what we had done had risen again in order to live in us to save us from what we are. He was a commanding, energetic, challenging man, very military in bearing but full of fun and utterly committed to reaching people, particularly young people, for Christ.

We had breakfast together, and he quickly outlined what he had in mind. He needed someone with business experience to handle finances—secretarial duties for the fellowship of young people who had visited the youth center, Capernwray Hall, where his ministry was based. It suddenly dawned on me that he was suggesting that I should leave my business career to deal with the business side of the ministry, whereas my thoughts had been to leave business to devote myself to preaching and reaching people. I felt deflated, and I'm afraid it showed. As he spoke about the burgeoning ministry of Torchbearers with his contagious enthusiasm I found that for me his offer was neither attractive nor contagious.

As he was jumping into his car, bound for the airport and New Zealand, I said, "I am grateful to you for thinking of me, but if you want an answer now I'm afraid it is no!" He was completely unperturbed by this and simply grinned, shook my hand, and said, "If the Lord Jesus wants you at Capernwray, you'll come; and if he doesn't, we don't want you anyway!" With that he roared off in the general direction of the Antipodes.

※※※※※※

The journey back to Manchester was strange. I had no doubt my banking days were numbered and the thought of working at Capernwray with Major Thomas, from whom Jill and I had derived so much spiritual help, had seemed so exciting and appealing. But I could not see any point in leaving a full-time responsible career in commerce and a full part-time ministry of preaching simply to do secretarial work and perhaps even cut back on my preaching. I needed to talk to Jill.

She was waiting to hear all about my visit, and she smiled when I recounted Major Thomas's parting words. "Typical," she said. We both had the deepest respect for his style and were greatly attracted to the exuberant, almost reckless abandon with which he approached life in general and ministry in particular. But "secretary of the fellowship" did not have any appeal at all.

"Well," said Jill, "Mr. Anderson will be here soon, and it looks as if we're going to the Pocket Testament League. Let's see what he says about housing. Don't forget our fleece!"

"I know all that, Jill. But Capernwray is so special to us. We know the people and they know us. I don't know much about Pocket Testament League—I've never even met Mr. Anderson yet. I'm confused!"

The said Mr. Anderson turned out to be a gentle, gracious giant of a man—successful in business, devoted in ministry in his spare time. He was a delight. We talked about all the possibilities of reaching out worldwide, and our hearts beat just a little faster as we talked. Surprisingly, he got into quite a lot of details, almost as if he was assuming we were going to join Pocket Testament League. But he never mentioned housing. We kept the conversation going long into the night hoping he would, but in the end we all went to bed tired and puzzled. Breakfast the next morning was hurried. Further brief conversation ensued, but not a word about housing. We parted, promising to pray for each other.

The next day the phone rang. "Good morning, Stuart. This is Van at Capernwray. Major Thomas just telephoned from New Zealand. He forgot to mention that if you decide God wants you at Capernwray, and we hope he does, you will live in Middle Lodge."

Was this coincidence? Was God guiding us? Was God using coincidence? Why would God guide me into something I didn't particularly want to do? All these questions and many more filled our minds for a number of weeks. Weeks filled with incredulous questions from bank colleagues. The young ones asking, "Why would you throw away a career?" The old ones wistfully saying, "I wish I had the guts to get out, but certainly not to become a minister."

As we talked with friends, searched the Scriptures, and prayed up a storm, the conviction slowly but separately developed in our hearts that we should go to Capernwray. But we were both very much afraid of overinfluencing each other, and we were totally convinced that both of us must sense God's call and guidance. It was not going to be a case of me being called and Jill being stuck with it.

One night we said to each other that it was time to bite the bullet. So we decided that at breakfast next morning we would each write on a piece of paper either "Capernwray" or "Pocket Testament League," then hand our paper to each other and open them simultaneously. I wrote on mine and handed my folded paper to Jill while she wrote on hers and handed it to me. "Okay," I said, "we'll open them on three." It all sounds overdone and overly dramatic thirty-three years later, but it seemed the most sensible thing in the world at the time. *What if she has written the other one?* I thought.

Quietly Jill said, "Are you ready? 1-2-3!"

"Capernwray" was written on both pieces of paper. We laughed, we hugged, we prayed, and we read together: "You shall go out with joy, and the trees of the field will clap their hands."

Immediately a vision of springtime at Capernwray— flowers, trees, blossoms, hordes of kids—filled our minds. With hardly a backward glance at the bank I loved and the city I enjoyed, we turned our eyes toward Capernwray and a new life. Together!

9

You Can't Buy This in a Shop

So this is the answer to our prayers, I thought as we examined the tiny picturesque lodge that stood at the gates that guarded the winding driveway up to Capernwray Hall. "It's beautiful, Stuart," I said with starry eyes. "Just look at the sweet little rooms. It will be cozy, don't you think?"

"The walls must be two feet thick," replied my pragmatic husband. "There's no room for anything but cozy in between them!"

"The rooms are rather small," I answered, "but never mind. Once the furniture is all in place, it will soon feel like home."

Capernwray Lodge belonged to Capernwray Hall, set at the doorway of the beautiful English lake district. The Hall was a sprawling country home that in bygone days had belonged to one family. Some of their servants had lived in a wing of the castlelike building, never coming beyond their designated areas of service. The family rooms were huge. It was hard to grasp how one family could utilize or justify all that living space—especially when one bedroom in one wing now slept twenty-five young people. But the atmosphere in the manor house that whispered of another world

101

in another day was wonderfully romantic, and we were delighted to put it to a more productive use.

The huge house had been used by the British army during the war years (World War II, in case any of you are wondering!). Major Ian Thomas and his lovely Irish wife, Joan, had bought it prior to the war to use for a Christian conference center. Serving with the British army in Germany at the end of the war, Major Thomas had a huge concern in his heart for the young Germans whose country and families had been decimated. Most of them had been trained in the Hitler youth movement, and their disillusionment was vast. He determined to invite them to Capernwray to introduce them to Christianity and win them for the Lord.

A few years later, his vision realized, the lovely old house rang with the sound of hundreds of young voices chattering in many languages as kids from all over the continent of Europe filled it to the rafters. We packed them into the dormitories. Some found themselves rubbing shoulders with the sons and daughters of their parents' war enemies.

I remember meeting a lovely young French girl who had been rounded up by the Nazis and, with her mother, forced to witness her father's death. Planting her bags on a bed at Capernwray, she greeted the girl next to her, discovering her companion to be German. Only in Christ could they become such wonderful friends. He who forgave the ones who hammered nails through his hands helped to heal the deep wounds, showing the young French girl how to forgive, though perhaps she would never be able to forget.

It was exciting. The staff consisted of a team of teachers and preachers, youth workers, and helpers with a love for the kids and an absolute dogged determination they should come to know and love Jesus Christ. They all worked extremely hard, counting themselves "on duty for the Lord"—as our leader put it—twenty-four hours of the day, seven days a week. Some of the leaders had formal theological training and others hadn't, but they all brought with them hands-on experience with youth. All lived on salaries considerably less than the employment benefits they had left behind, but they had learned to share with each other whatever came their way.

"God promised us our daily bread," I said to Stuart.

"True enough," he replied, "but we're going to need to remember he didn't promise us the butter and jam as well!"

I had reason to remember that remark in the years to come. For example, we were to live in property that was not our own. Middle Lodge belonged, as did all the other properties on the grounds of Capernwray, to the missionary fellowship of which we were a part. We were to learn that everyone treated mission property, which included our house, as their own. This was community living, and it was going to be a big adjustment for all of us. It's one thing to live in a house and decide who to invite in on your terms, but an entirely different thing to have people invite themselves in on their terms!

Running up the tiny narrow staircase of Middle Lodge the day we arrived, I was somewhat surprised to be met by a smiling face attached to a solid-looking young man at the top of the stairs.

"Hullo, I'm Klaus," he said with a heavy accent. "I work at the Hall as a carpenter, and I live here."

"So do we," I blurted out.

"That's nice," he replied with a huge grin. So saying, he turned away into one of the tiny bedrooms!

Oh dear, I thought, *maybe no one told him we were coming.* I followed him into the room (it took all of three steps from the top of the stairs) and said, "Klaus, our whole family has come to live at Middle Lodge."

"Please?" he inquired pleasantly. I learned later that *bitte* can mean "please" or the equivalent of "I beg your pardon" in English or "huh" in American. I didn't have the heart to go on. Smiling lamely I excused myself and ran downstairs to find my husband, leaving Klaus wondering why saying "Please?" would make a woman run away.

"He'll leave—don't worry. We'll talk to him later," Stuart said, hearing me out as he heaved boxes into the house. But Klaus was nowhere to be found "later." Tired out with the move, we tumbled into sleeping bags, deciding to tackle the problem of our unexpected lodger the next morning.

As I put breakfast on the table the following day, Klaus appeared. "I like living with you very much," he said with a charming twinkle in his eye, and before I could catch my breath and say a thing he disappeared up to the Hall, telling me he would eat up there as he could see we weren't unpacked yet! I certainly hadn't bargained on this. A week later he was still firmly ensconced in our little lodge, and I must say, even though we had really come to like him around the place, there was certainly "no room at the inn."

"We've got to tell him he has to go," Stuart said reluctantly and proceeded to do just that. Klaus took the news cheerfully enough and went to pack. As baths and showers were at a premium in the dormitory to which he was now assigned, he decided to take a last, leisurely hot bath. At this moment a friend arrived to help us by doing some electrical work. Without me realizing it, he began to fix a faulty immersion heater switch outside the bathroom. Klaus, heartily singing and splashing, accompanied our friend's determined hammering. Suddenly there was a blinding flash as the amateur electrician's screwdriver slipped (he had failed to turn off the electricity). The electrician was hurled violently across the room and Klaus's singing stopped dead. "Oh, no," I howled, "we've electro-cuted Klaus!"

Fortunately, even though Klaus was sitting in a tub of water that was attached to the offending immersion heater, we only had one casualty: the amateur electrician who was severely shocked. But we did also have one German guest who suddenly became extremely eager to move out of Middle Lodge as soon as possible! So then at last we were alone.

A few days later our furniture arrived from Manchester. We tugged and pushed, squeezed and shoved all day long till most of our things were in place. A minor problem arose when we tried to get our bed up the tiny staircase, which had a right-angle bend at the bottom. The box mattress refused to make the turn. The windows of the bedroom refused to open wide enough to admit its entrance, so I left Stuart, Klaus, and the helpers to solve the problem while I went food shopping. When I came back, Klaus told me the bed was safely installed in the tiny bedroom, and the fact that the door couldn't close with the bed in the room didn't seem to bother Stuart at all.

"We always sleep with our eyes closed," my husband offered cheerfully. I wondered what that had to do with anything.

"How did you manage to get it up the stairs?" I asked.

"Easy," my husband responded. "I found the perfect solution. It may take a little patching up, but it's up there!"

Running upstairs with an ominous feeling, I discovered that Stuart had taken a knife and cut the mattress completely in two! I spent the rest of the afternoon sewing his "perfect solution" together and wondering why I had gone shopping.

The next crisis arose when someone decided the chimney should be swept. "Don't you think it might make a mess now that everything's in place?" I asked somewhat nervously.

"Oh, no problem," my husband answered cheerily. "Old John, the groundskeeper who lives at High Lodge, said he'll help. He's got some brushes."

"But you've never swept a chimney, Stuart," I objected. "Isn't that sort of a difficult thing to do?"

"We have to do this sort of thing ourselves now, Jill," Stuart explained. "We can't afford to pay people to do things like we used to. It's amazing what you can do if you have to. Anyway, it can't be too difficult. All you do is shove the brush up and pull it down again."

So saying, up on the roof went old John, and into the tiny fireplace, and up the chimney went the brush, pushed firmly in the direction of heaven by my husband. I watched, fascinated, with the baby dangling over my arm.

"It's stuck," Stuart shouted up the twisted chimney.

"Don't fuss yourself," John's voice came back cheerfully. "I know what'll move it—hang on." He climbed off the old roof, fetched a brick, and dropped it down the chimney to dislodge the obstruction. *Thud* went the brick, bounding down the twisting chimney. The banging stopped abruptly. Stuart peered in the hearth. "It's stuck!" he shouted for the second time.

"Don't fuss yourself. I know what to do," responded our "expert" as he perched precariously on top of the now totally clogged-up chimney. Climbing down, he merrily set about cutting down a holly bush. "This time you go on the roof, Stuart, and drop a rope down the chimney," John ordered.

He then tied the rope to the holly bush and shouted to Stuart, "Pull as hard as you can. That should shift it."

It didn't. In fact, the holly bush joined the brush and the brick halfway up the chimney. "It's stuck," shouted my intrepid husband—for the third time.

I bet he'll make up a wonderful illustration about this next time he preaches, I thought grimly. *If he says anything about a bush, a brush, and a brick, I will not be responsible for my reactions.*

John seemed perfectly happy. My heart sank. *Oh, no,* I thought. *Stuart has found another optimist just like himself.*

"I know the answer," John shouted up the chimney.

"What are you going to do?" I inquired, becoming alarmed.

"We'll light a fire in the grate and burn the bush, which will set fire to the brush, and that should bring the brick down," he answered simply. So saying, he set fire to the paper. The bush, however, wasn't the only thing that was on fire. The soot caught, too, and the brick, still firmly lodged in place, choked the draught and sent thick black smoke back into our lovely, clean, newly painted house— and into our eyes and throats.

What a start, I thought grimly. *That's our only means of heating in the whole house, and now it's blocked by a brick!*

In the eight years we lived in Middle Lodge we never could get the fire going properly, and the brick, as far as I know, is still there!

"Is this what Christian work is all about?" I asked my husband. "Do we have to do things in such an amateurish way?"

"Not necessarily," Stuart replied, "but we can't afford professionals now. It's another small adjustment we'll have to make." I wondered if I was ready for this.

What wouldn't we be able to afford? I mused. What furniture could we buy for our house? Would we be able to purchase a car? Some members of the team couldn't. It was going to be embarrassing to depend on others to get us places. We were in the middle of the country, with no public transportation. I didn't want our children to be under-dressed when they went to school, or not be able to go to extracurricular activities, and I wondered how I would manage to curtail my urge to buy new clothes—an urge that up to now hadn't been a problem at all, since the funds had always been readily available.

"The Lord keeps you humble and the brethren keep you poor in this business," a colleague laughed when we talked about it together. "But the dividends God gives are price-less," he added as a quiet afterthought.

I think it was harder on Stuart than on me. He thought of all he would have been able to provide for us if he had not given up his career, but the privilege of our environment vastly outweighed the material considerations we were tempted to consider. When the neighborhood kids were given bikes for Christmas, or friends were able to afford a vacation when we couldn't, we made mental lists of the things that didn't cost money that were ours for the taking.

Our three children (Judy and Pete had joined our team by now) were constantly exposed to wonderful young people from multiple backgrounds and cultures and acquired hun-dreds of aunts and uncles, big sisters and brothers over-night. They were also playing with little friends who belonged to committed Christian parents. They couldn't help absorbing principles from the atmosphere of those loving relationships. They were around adults who were living sacrificially for others. "You can't buy that in a shop," I commented to Stuart.

"And just look at our backyard, Jill," my husband responded. "The garden is fabulous. One hundred and six acres of prime woods and parkland dotted with magnificent chestnuts, beeches, and oaks. There are rivers to fish and animals to see—rabbits, birds, and foxes. And just think about the incredible highland cattle with their wild horns splayed out like coat racks."

"And there are berries to pick and eat, and flowers that only an English garden can produce almost all year round. All these things are ours free," I added.

And think of all our children will see as Christ changes people's lives, I thought. Where else could they observe so much of God's transforming power shown in human behavior? How else could the kids ever really know the most important thing in life is to obey Christ and follow him where he leads, whatever the cost, if we weren't doing it here together? You can't put a price tag on that! Then it didn't seem to matter anymore. The best things in life are surely free. We would do the best we could with the resources we were given.

We began to see God provide for us almost as soon as we had unpacked. German and Swiss teenagers wanted to learn English in a home setting and so came to Capernwray to be *au pair* girls. We opened up the room Klaus had vacated, packed the three kids into one small bedroom, and invited a succession of these young women to join our family. We shared companionship, benefitted from their helping hands, and made lasting friendships. We shared our home and food, and they gave us a few hours of domestic help, releasing us (me in particular) to do other things.

One of those things involved taking groups of English youngsters to the Continent for two-week house parties. I was excited to be asked to be in charge of sixty kids who were going to Holland. Stuart, who would be preaching in Germany,. was to meet us at our destination. It sounded easy enough and quite an adventure. It didn't seem to me that much could go wrong. Little did I know! I had one party ticket for all of us, which didn't help when we boarded the boat, as half the party was let through the line onto the vessel while the other half didn't make it. Standing heroically on the gangplank, clutching the ropes on either side of me, I resisted all attempts by officials to dislodge me until my whole group was intact and on board. At last, cheered on by the kids, we triumphantly set sail. I soon discovered how sixty lively English kids can think up umpteen ways to mess up the system within less time than it takes to invent it. The boat journey from Dover to Ostende was terrible. The ferry was so crowded there was nowhere for us to sit but the deck, and my group, not wanting to sit anyway, scattered immediately. I spent the whole crossing climbing over bodies trying to find them all. The kids had a ball playing hide-and-go-seek with me.

On arriving in Belgium we promptly boarded the wrong train, as no one could understand one word of Flemish. Fortunately, we discovered our mistake before setting off in the direction of Germany, and eventually we arrived at the youth center hours and hours late. "Where've you been?" my husband greeted me, grinning. I didn't answer, which was just as well! We were treated to a warm Dutch welcome and a supper of yogurt and chocolate chips, which our kids promptly refused to eat. "Call this supper, do you?" they asked. "Where's the fish and chips?" Others were struggling with culture shock. "Why don't these people speak English?" asked one bemused youngster. "The place is full of foreigners," offered a freckle-faced girl in response.

Yes, it was an experience, but once settled in beautiful Wassenaar we adjusted and had a wonderful time of fun and fellowship. We saw many of those bright youngsters ask for God's forgiveness and receive it, becoming new people as he promised. It was wonderful. "You can't buy all that in a store," I murmured happily in my husband's ear.

And so our first years of adjustment at Middle Lodge were filled out. They were good years, growing years, when we found our family footings, establishing a routine that made a priority of spiritual responsibilities. "As for me and my house," we had promised, "we will serve the Lord." Our kids never knew anything different. As far as they were concerned, that's what life was all about—serving the Lord—serving him from before breakfast until late at night, and even through the night if a kid needed help or an adult needed encouragement. In the morning, afternoon, and evening we served him. In the kitchen, the playground, the park, and at nursery school, service was a way of life. And even when no one was watching at all, save God himself, we tried to put out 100 percent.

Part of that service was to each other, of course. I realized I was just as surely serving the Lord when I ironed Stuart's shirts, played peek-a-boo with my baby, roughhoused with my toddler, or read a story to our oldest, as when I was teaching Sunday school or reaching teenagers for Christ. Three kids were a heap of work—but a happy, holy heap as far as I was concerned.

The family is a fantastic place to develop a servant spirit. The gift of our children provided an abundant workshop to hone those skills. Judy and Pete were born at daffodil and rhododendron time. Stuart had been amazed when Judy was born. Not, I hasten to add, because he was a stranger to the process, but because he didn't believe he could produce a girl. Years later I wrote about that in a book dedicated to Judy:

> Thank you for being a girl. You were a shock to your dad. He didn't believe he could produce one of our kind! I could see the bewilderment in his face as you lay snugly in his arms. "Whatever shall I do with one of these?" he asked me silently. You knew, didn't you? You knew that, man that he was from a man's world, he needed to learn what a woman was all about. Thank you for teaching him—he's loved it!
>
> Thank you for being a tomboy. For falling off the donkey and joining in the football, and keeping up with every brother-step along the way. I tried to get you interested in dolls, but you just thumped your friends with them.
>
> Thank you for coming to Christ. I can still see your sticky candy hands clutching at my baking board, your big blue eyes in a still point of their own, wondering if Jesus would want you to put your toys away if you let him into your heart. I remember! Thank you for coming anyway even when I told you yes about the toys. Thank you for loving the Lord I love!
>
> Jill Briscoe, *Thank You for Being a Friend* (Grand Rapids, Mich.: Zondervan, 1980)

Once born, Judy walked into her daddy's life, took up residence in his heart, and changed him forever.

Our youngest, Pete, who arrived three weeks late, learned from his earliest days that number three's lot in life is to be generally ignored by Mom and Dad, who are too busy with numbers one and two to pay too much attention to him. He seemed to accept with good humor his treatment by numbers one and two, which consisted of being mercilessly beat up on, as a matter of course. He soon discovered he needed to develop a laid-back, philosophical, kind of fatalistic attitude to life in order to survive, and a fun-loving, happy-go-lucky personality in order for life to have purpose and meaning. Having achieved these goals from his youngest days, Pete settled down with great grace and humor to bring himself up!

David continued his steady progress toward his future vocation of shepherding God's flock by trying seriously to round up Judy and Pete with whatever rod or staff lay at hand—and to tidy them up a bit. Dave could never stand anything out of place. His heavenly Father was a God of orderliness, and Dave couldn't abide Judy and Pete messing up the system.

Life was all joy. Our three precious little bundles gave us all an incredible sense of belonging, truly a legacy from the Lord. Our children all came to know Christ before they were six years of age. They asked their four- and five-year-old questions and as best they knew how, told Jesus they wanted him in their hearts—and God answered those big prayers from those little people. I know he did. I saw the difference as Judy picked up her toys, David said sorry to Pete, and Pete bore his station in life gamely.

Our family was together for a few short years, and we made the most of every moment. We packed the minutes with fun and laughter, play and serious thoughts. It was as if we knew it couldn't last for long.

And God had something new in mind for all of us.

10

On the Road Again,
Again, and Again

Stuart

The first few months in our new situation were not easy. At Capernwray we had spent many wonderful, carefree vacation days, but we were no longer on vacation—we had arrived to work. I think we had also come to our new environment "trailing clouds of glory." The bank people had told us repeatedly how much they admired what we were doing in giving up a career, but at Capernwray everybody had already done something similar. Major Thomas had walked away from medical school years earlier, Mr. Van-Dooren had been a successful real-estate agent, Billy Strachan had been in show business, and John Hunter had been a school principal. So what we were secretly regarding as *sacrifice* was perfectly unremarkable to them.

Then, of course, we had run into the old problem of unrealistic expectations. We were, after all, in full-time service—the phrase had a magical ring to it; the concept held a certain grand mystique. The reality, however, was that full-time Christian service had a very thin veneer of glamour to it and a lot of hard work, long hours, tired people, inadequate resources, and strained relationships slightly below the surface.

We had gone to Capernwray convinced that it was the place of God's choosing but confused about why he had chosen it. Preaching and teaching were the desires of my heart, but I found myself, at first, doing very little of either and a great deal of office work—most of it at a level that I had long since left behind in the bank. In addition, I soon discovered that when the sewers got blocked or the chimneys needed sweeping they were the responsibility of whoever was around at the time. So I pitched in with a show of enthusiasm, a desire to meet expectations, and a marked lack of expertise.

Eventually, I was invited to preach to some of the teenagers who came to special conferences, and so I thought I was beginning to hit my stride. Then something most unexpected happened. I, who had had rarely a day's illness, contracted a throat infection that would not go away. At first I was not at all concerned. But when eventually I asked a doctor to check it out, he told me that I needed complete rest, no talking in ordinary conversation, and, of course, absolutely no public speaking. He added a particularly sobering warning that I might lose my voice permanently. For a few weeks I was housebound, left to my thoughts, and—for the first time in my life—depressed. Jill was concerned. But as I tried, unsuccessfully, to keep my own counsel, she worked hard at putting our little home together and settling our little boy in his new environment.

One day as I was contemplating a career I no longer had, a new career I didn't particularly want, and the possibility that the only thing I wanted to do—preach—might be gone forever, I prayed one of the most common and the most heartfelt and the briefest prayers known to man—"Why?" I didn't hear a voice and I didn't see a vision, but I did get an answer: *"You ask, 'Why?' I'll tell you. It's to see if you love preaching about the Lord more than you love the Lord about whom you preach!"*

That, as they say, was heavy stuff. But I confronted it, wrestled with it, and finally answered, "Lord, if I never preach again I promise you I'll still love you and serve you. But, please, I really would like to preach!" This was another turning point that allowed me to discover pride and self-centeredness, an exaggerated view of my own importance, and a number of other obvious things that I would have denied vehemently under less revealing and incontrovertible circumstances. As you may have guessed, my throat problem cleared up, and despite constant use and abuse for more than three decades, the problem has never recurred. I'm grateful that I was graciously allowed to learn some of these lessons in the early days of full-time service!

As I worked with the young people who passed through the youth center, I began to do a little more preaching and a lot of counseling. I made many friendships, and before long I was encouraged to accept the invitations that came my way to visit the youth clubs and churches from which these kids had come. In time this meant traveling over the channel to the European continent, bidding Jill and the baby frequent good-byes.

I would be less than honest if I denied that there was not a considerable degree of excitement and ego involved in the travel, but there was also much evidence that God was mightily at work in young people's lives all over Europe and he was allowing me to be a part of it. I didn't have much trouble keeping on top of my office responsibilities, and Major Thomas said approvingly that my desk was more often graced by my absence than my presence. My home was also becoming more graced by absence than presence, but I did not give a lot of thought to it. And when the thought did occur to me, I consoled myself with the words of Christ about his disciples having to love him more than family.

Trips to glamour spots like the Swiss Alps, Norwegian fjords, Swedish lakes, and cosmopolitan places like Berlin, Warsaw, and Prague called me. Always there were young people to minister to, always there were signs of blessing, always there were more opportunities than time to fill them. It was exciting and challenging and wonderfully fulfilling. Jill and I talked about me being away and decided that if the Lord was calling us to be living this way he would certainly equip us for it. So we pressed on: Jill in her small corner and I in my ever-expanding one. As the years went by David was joined first by Judy and later by Peter. One of our friends who was not totally in favor of my protracted absences, on observing our growing family sniffed, "Well, I see you managed to get home twice!"

On one occasion I was in Wuppertal, Germany, concluding a series of meetings and preparing to drive through East Germany to Berlin when I got a phone call from our family doctor, an old man who cared for all the staff at Capernwray. He made no Christian profession, describing himself as a God-fearing agnostic, and he had once confided to Jill that he was terrified of dying. I was surprised to hear his voice on the other end of the line.

"Stuart," he said, "I know you Capernwray people stop at nothing serving the Lord, and I know you are prepared to forgo a lot of things for the sake of your ministry. But you need to know that Jill is ill. She doesn't want you to know because she doesn't want to stop you going to Berlin, but I'm telling you that she needs you more than the kids in Berlin need you, so get yourself home at once if not sooner, and I want to see you in my office in two days. You see, your wife has a heart bigger than her body, and you and I have got to work out what to do about her. I'm telling you to get yourself home!"

Times have changed dramatically. Now we have books that suggest that missionaries like C. T. Studd and J. Hudson Taylor neglected their families, but in those days we had books about the same gentlemen, extolling the way they took up their crosses and followed Christ. These days we hear about the primacy of the family; in those days we believed in the primacy of the ministry. In those days we were told stories of missionaries' kids being baptized by their fathers' murderers. Today we read of missionaries refusing to be separated from their children. I suggest the pendulum has swung as far to one extreme now as it was to the other extreme in those days.

It is quite possible, therefore, that the modern reader may find it incomprehensible that I hesitated about canceling the balance of my trip and returning home to my wife. I was not in the habit of canceling anything, and neither were my colleagues. In fact, we were convinced that if in show business, "the show must go on"—in the King's business it was even more important it should continue. But I canceled the trip to Berlin, despite the objection of the young man from New Zealand who was traveling with me, and we returned home. Jill cried when she saw me. She was physically exhausted, emotionally drained, but mainly concerned that she was hindering the work of the Lord in my life "by being so weak"!

With the help of our wonderful physician we began to learn some things about balancing family and ministry. It was ironic that he, from his basically humanistic yet sympathetic perspective, was able to see things more clearly than we were able to see them. He showed Jill that being *submissive* did not mean being *stupid,* and he showed me that being *committed* did not mean being *callous*. He helped Jill to see that "her God," as he called him, was smart enough to give her a body capable of doing what needed doing, and therefore, if it began to complain, it was "her God's" way of getting her attention and demanding some changes. He also told me that if I thought I was "head" of the family it was about time I accepted more responsibility for it. He got our attention—we listened and we tried to adjust. Over the years we learned much from this dear man. We love him, and we know that in his gruff, undemonstrative way he loved us and respected the One we served, despite his doubts.

▰▰▰▰▰▰

So the years went by, full, busy, and blessed. Then one day Major Thomas returned from a tour of ministry in the U.S.A. and announced that he had so many invitations that he could not fulfill them. He had, therefore, recommended my name, the people had accepted his suggestion, and I would be leaving shortly for three months in the States. The thought was at once exciting and disconcerting. I had met many Americans as they had passed through our center and had so often had to help them adjust to the lifestyle we offered them since it apparently differed dramatically from what they were accustomed to. If that was the case, I thought, I would not only have to adjust to their culture, but I would be expected to say something relevant to people living a lifestyle I didn't even understand.

I asked one of my colleagues who was familiar with the American scene, "Can you give me some tips about ministry in America?" He had answered not very helpfully, although accurately, "Sure, wear plenty of deodorant. Americans like that."

Major Thomas's comment had been about as succinct, although of a more spiritual orientation. When I had protested that I felt overwhelmed by the weight of responsibility he was placing on me he replied, "Jesus Christ in you is adequate—so get on with it." So, armed with my best sermons, plenty of deodorant, and an almost desperate conviction that Christ was adequate even though I was not, I said good-bye—this time for three months.

Part of the reason for my trepidation was that I was going to be sharing ministry with men to whom I had been listening for years. I loved Stephen Olford's clearly outlined exposition of Scripture; I always got excited listening to Alan Redpath's fiery, energetic preaching; and Paul Ree's cultured, gentlemanly approach to life showed through his preaching so clearly that I had been deeply challenged by him to enlarge my understanding and vision. And now I would be sharing ministry with them, not sitting in the crowd listening to them.

Incidentally, they all greatly encouraged me. Stephen called me "my boy" and still does. Alan would whisper before I preached, "K.O.K.D.," which I knew meant "Keep on kicking the devil." And Paul, to my intense embarrassment, sat in the front row taking notes.

I was thrust into an exciting world of large churches, enthusiastic crowds, generous, even lavish, hospitality, and many of the delightful experiences that the United States offered a young man from a small town in the north of England.

On many days I preached on seven different occasions. I was invited as a guest on TV shows, preached on radio, and was interviewed by newspapers, featured in magazines, and told repeatedly, "We love your accent!" People hugged me when I least expected it, fed me when I least needed it, put me in the limelight when I was least ready for it, and generally swept me along at a fast and furious pace. I took to America like a duck to water. Repeatedly invited to return, I found my diary filling up for another tour of ministry long before I had completed the first one.

Jill wrote long letters telling me about the children and the small details of life in the family, while I wrote long letters describing my initial perceptions: supermarkets (beautiful, colorful emporiums designed for extorting money painlessly), college football (rugby with a helmet, with bands and bears running around and pretty girls in swimsuits for some inexplicable reason twirling swords around their necks, and ministers praying no one would get hurt), churches (spacious, comfortable, superbly equipped sanctuaries with acres of parking lots that never seemed big enough), and America (a country run by women for children at men's expense).

It did occur to me that Jill's letters spoke often about missing me and the children asking about me, but I didn't say much about that sort of thing because I was so busy from morning till night that I had little time to think about home. As each week of ministry climaxed and concluded, I had the excitement of jumping on the plane, arriving in a new city, meeting new people, and starting all over again.

I didn't realize what was happening at the time, but subsequently I recognized that I, like so many young men when confronted with professional opportunity, had simply responded to the opportunity and assumed the family would keep pace. My situation was complicated in that my motivation, genuine service, and commitment to the cause of Christ also contained elements of selfishness and pride, adventurism and status. If anyone had asked me at the time, "What makes you keep going at such a rate?" I would have answered quite truthfully, "A sense of divine calling." And if anyone asked, as they did occasionally, "How can you be a father and gone from your family so much?" I would have countered, "How can I be an international evangelist and stay at home?"

Meanwhile Jill, as she put it, was trying to be Mom and Dad to our little family.

※※※※※※

At times pangs of loneliness, even in the midst of supportive crowds, would come over me. I was made to feel at home by so many wonderful people who to this day number among our most cherished friends. Their homes became a home away from home. On the rare occasions when I had a break in my schedule I could stay for a day or two, catch up on laundry, kick off my shoes, and have a leisurely chat. But it wasn't home, and they weren't Jill, David, Judy, and Peter. The worst moments for me were passing through an airport and seeing a British Airways jet getting ready to leave for London. I would stand and look at it, realizing that if I got on board I would be in England before morning. More than once I had to take myself in hand, turn away, and carry on with my itinerary.

The commitments that Jill and I had made before the Lord were so solid that there was never a hint of estrangement and never the slightest thought of alienation, but I suspect there were traces of distance. Not a lack of love or a diminishing of commitment or even a suspicion of unfaithfulness, but I had struck out on my own, and I suppose Jill had tried to compensate by filling the space I had left with things and projects and people. We became aware of this after one of my tours of ministry.

I had been away for three months and had spoken literally hundreds of times. On arriving home I discovered that Jill had filled the house with ladies she had been ministering to, and she expected me to speak to them. I pointed out to her (in the kitchen, out of earshot) that I had enough meetings to last me for a while, and I had been flying all night and had more interest in going to bed than in teaching Romans 6, and how could she be so thoughtless? To which she replied that it would be nice if I didn't forget dear old England while I was rushing around the world, and she would appreciate it if I would show a little interest in the work she was doing, but if that was how I felt she would do it herself and I could go to bed!

After three months apart this was hardly the type of reunion we had looked forward to! But it served to show that the "distance" was there, the different interests were beginning to compete, and a lack of mutual sensitivity had resulted.

I, of course, did not go to bed. I taught Romans 6 to the ladies, and they said how grateful they were that I had done it even though they were sure I must be tired. I said, "Oh, not at all; it was a pleasure," and Jill and I shared one of those special, private looks across the room. After the ladies had gone home Jill and I quickly did what we've always been able to do—deal with a problem and get on with living. But both of us had seen signals we could not ignore. We, who had been made one, were in danger of growing apart.

One of the things we were able to do was to arrange for Jill to join me on a tour of ministry for a few weeks. The children were well cared for, Jill needed a change of pace, and we needed to share ministry together again. I remember picking her up at the airport in Philadelphia. She had bought a new suit complete with gloves and hat (very English), which she soon discovered were not exactly ideal for the oppressive Philadelphia heat.

Anyway, I got her into the car, switched on the air conditioning (a novelty for Jill that in later years became a necessity), and we set out for our destination. I was excited about showing her the sights and explaining everything I knew, but she was not particularly interested. Assuming she was tired and jet-lagged, I decided she needed silence more than anything else. Little did I know that she was beginning to feel the effects of a migraine headache, the first of a series which bedeviled her the whole time she was with me on the trip. This, coupled with a long-standing inordinate fear of flying, made life pretty miserable for her and accordingly for me!

What was supposed to be a dream trip turned out to have many characteristics of a nightmare. Our itinerary took us from Philadelphia to Florida to California to Vancouver to Toronto and included many magnificent sights and wonderful times of ministry. Jill had her good days but was rarely herself, and I was struggling to meet the demands of ministry and the needs of a sick wife. Matters got even worse when we received a message that Judy had had an accident and was in the hospital but okay. We had every confidence in the ones caring for her, but the heartstrings were twanging loudly and clearly.

Given the difficulties of the trip it was therefore a total surprise to me to hear Jill say as she was boarding her return flight to England, "I don't know what this means, but I believe God has called us to North America!" With that her flight was called, she flew off, I got back to the rest of my itinerary, and once again I marveled at my wife. During a very difficult time, in less than ideal circumstances, she had sensed a calling that eventually proved correct while I, as usual, was to catch on much later. Though I had no idea what she was talking about, I had by this time learned to take very seriously any and all statements she made that she believed were prompted by the Spirit.

A number of happy, busy, fruitful years would unfold before the full impact of her initial sense of calling came to fulfillment, but she had, once again, opened my mind and heart to a possibility I had not previously entertained.

11

The Daddy Space

"I've been asked to visit America," Stuart told me one day.

"Oooo," said David, "where's that?"

"It's far away across the sea," Stuart answered him. It all sounded very exciting and challenging.

"How long will you be gone?" I asked casually.

"Not too long—just three months," he replied.

"Just three months!" I gasped. It seemed an awfully long haul to me at the time, but the excitement of the opportunity to take a tour of speaking engagements set up for him by Major Thomas, who himself had a worldwide ministry, quieted my misgivings. *It's just for experience,* I told myself. *It will soon be over.*

My husband didn't tell me till years later that Major Thomas had said to him, "I don't know if I should have done this because I have a feeling you will never come back if I send you over there." If I had known that, I would have been a lot more apprehensive. Anyway, the kids and I packed him up and sent him off with a wing and a prayer, and I planned an especially packed schedule to wile away the time he was gone.

Three months later he came home with a wonderful report about his warm reception and dozens of invitations to return the following year for more meetings.

I remember thinking, *Oh no, we left the bank and came to Capernwray so we could be together. If we'd wanted to have a traveling ministry we could have chosen another missionary society.* I thought back to the way we had so carefully picked this particular opening and how it had seemed the ideal place to live happily ever after with our little family. Had we mistaken the track? Had we lost our way in the forest?

The first part of the following year, Stuart set off once more on a three-month stint in the U.S.A., returning to tell me how he felt it had been right to commit himself to three more months abroad at the end of the year as well. "That's six months," I said. "That's tough." We looked at each other. We both knew the tough bit would be toughed out if necessary. The thing we had to figure out was if it was necessary. Was this God's plan? Was this what he had in mind before the world began? If so, we would go ahead. I remember reading Psalm 139:16—"All the days ordained for me were written in your book before one of them came to be"—and I wasn't about to edit God's writing!

I tried not to think too much about it and busied myself, staying excited about the wonderful doors of opportunity that were opening for Stuart. Meanwhile I worked hard at keeping the children part of it all. Up on the wall went a map of America with "Stuart's Missionary Journey" written across the top of it. We colored and cut out little paper airplanes which I explained were St. Stuart's "air donkeys." I'm sure the comparison with St. Paul and my husband was quite lost on our kids since they were so young, but we had fun sticking air donkeys over all the places Daddy was visiting, and we prayed for him. It didn't seem to bother the little ones that their dad was seemingly in Cuba (my geography is abysmal; actually he was in Florida!). They certainly missed him and loved the reunions at Manchester Airport, after which we would all take off to the zoo or the fairground to celebrate his return.

Bigger questions were demanding answers now. "How can Stuart fulfill his fathering role and be away all the time?" a good friend asked me with genuine concern. I had to admit she was putting my own questions into words. "How can he fulfill the evangelist's role and stay home all the time?" countered the quiet, serene voice of a visiting missionary who happened to be there when the hard question was asked. Of course, I ruminated later, he couldn't be home if his work could only be done when he was away. Not being God, he didn't have the ability to be omnipresent!

That thought gave me a sharp reminder. He wasn't God. He was my wonderful and much-loved earthly husband, and I had learned (or thought I had learned) years before that I was to lean on my heavenly husband and not my earthly one. Then again, God was God and seeing he was omnipotent, he would be my "El Shaddai," the one who would be all I would need as the occasion arose. He had promised.

"How do you keep the ministry from intruding into your family life?" an earnest young pastor's wife asked me not too long ago. I paused before I gave her an answer, thinking back to those ten learning years. "The ministry isn't an enemy—a rival lover—snatching away quality time from the family," I replied. "When you talk like that, it's as if you are saying, 'Jesus is intruding into our lives.' Jesus and ministry are the same thing to me."

It's funny—I never had a problem with bitterness toward the mission for creating our situation. I only had a problem adjusting to the disappointments I was experiencing. But I did have a problem. The whole thing was not turning out according to plan: my plan. First of all, I had this idealistic notion that ministry was a glamorous thing; that all missionaries were near perfect people; that missionary kids were all little angels; and—the biggest misconception of all—I would take to the rigors of missionary life like a duck takes to water. Well, I was discovering this duck didn't like the missionary duck pond.

The first struggle I had was to learn to struggle in secret. Like a certain king in the Old Testament, I discovered people seemed to find out the very words we (Stuart and I) spoke to each other in the privacy of our bedchamber. Living together in community had more problems than the initial ones we had encountered with Klaus and our bathroom! Our business became everyone's business, and everyone's business became ours. Godly gossip flew faster than the ungodly sort. If I had said one little thing about my feelings, within a short time all sorts of folks would approach me with verses of Scripture, loving hugs, murmured promises to pray for me, or knowing looks. This was particularly hard as my struggles would begin in earnest as soon as Stuart went away. I had to let it all out to someone.

I had never been much of one for having a best friend. In fact, I had never been one for having any friends. I had—as I have already told—been far too selfish an individual to build good friendships. Now, for the first time in my life, I realized I needed the comfortable companionship of someone other than my husband. A woman friend. God supplied that need in the person of a lovely girl who came for a week's holiday and stayed at Capernwray for the next thirty years! Angela was full of fun, creative, a very bright new Christian, and brimming over with adventure. She was my Jonathan, strengthening my hand in the Lord when I was ready to pack it all in, and my Nathan, making me face up to reality and get on with the job at hand. She loved our kids and became a favorite aunt, and she loved me and became a friend such as I have never had before or since. Together we laughed, shared, cried, and began to reach out of ourselves to the people in our area.

There were lonely, bored young teens around, and we started a youth club for them on Friday nights. Soon we outgrew the days of the week and all the hours in the day with busy, happy happenings. There were lonely old ladies too—hidden behind the thatched roofs, climbing trellises of fragrant English roses, and whitewashed cottage walls— who were shyly appreciative of the invitation to visit our little cottages and hear about Christ. Loneliness can be an empty space reverberating with self-pity or a full place packed with other lonely people.

Now I had someone with whom I could share and trust my confidences. And someone who was not afraid to say the hard things when they needed saying. "You're not the only lonely person on earth, Jilly," Angela once told me cheerfully. "At least you have three gorgeous kids and a husband that comes back at least twice a year. There are lots of us single girls (unclaimed treasures, Stuart's father used to call them) who are really alone."

It was true. And then I thought about my husband. What was he feeling? How selfish of me to be so self-absorbed. He was far more alone than I was. He surely must be longing for a rough-and-tumble with his little boys. Did he dream about the joy of holding his little girl close and reading her a favorite story when she was pink and warm, bathed and ready for bed? Suddenly I was overwhelmingly thankful for them all. That night, for the first time, I wept for my husband's empty spaces instead of weeping for mine.

Angie was right: None of us was as alone as she was. I watched her love Jesus thoroughly and completely, giving her singleness to the One who himself chose that way of life. Her particular struggles were better known to him than to anyone else on earth. I understood a very little of the great love and appreciation God must have for her, and I thanked her for being such a faithful friend.

Loneliness is still an unwelcome guest, but looking back I know it affords me space to develop friendships and ministry skills I would never develop any other way. Take speaking, for instance. Women didn't speak in those days. Well, not in church, that is. If they did have some part of a church service, it was to be called sharing, not preaching or speaking—that being men's prerogative. To share, however, apparently gave the activity a kosher stamp of approval. I had been aware that most of the church fellowships I had visited used their women in serving rather than in speaking or authority roles. Stuart had been raised to believe women must be silent in the church. It was neither seemly nor scripturally acceptable for a woman to do such things, his church leaders had said.

At first I had been amazed at such—in my humble opinion—archaic ideas, but having been shown some pretty straightforward texts and been told "The Bible says it, you must believe it, and that settles it," I had more or less accepted this fact as something I needed to submit to. I decided it would do my proud heart good to buckle under and do what I was told.

I was a teacher—a good one, I had been told—so I knew that I could speak. As opportunities came I simply began to use all my trained skills to teach the Bible, thoroughly enjoying such spiritual activity, and with apparent effectiveness. Here and there a Methodist church (which seemed to put women in their pulpits without a problem) or university campus would ask me to take a service, and I complied, with a little trepidation because of the "submission" thing.

Once or twice a man (often a leader in the church) would come up to me at the end and say something like, "I don't think women should speak in church." Since they usually waited till I had just finished doing exactly that, I was usually at a loss to know how to respond. After all, they had invited me to do it in the first place. Not a few times the man would add, "I was surprised—you were good." Well, that was stranger still! It was as if they felt since I shouldn't be doing it, I shouldn't be good. I could see some were genuinely questioning their beliefs about the matter, but it certainly threw me for a loop.

Once when I timidly offered that I felt it was all right to teach, seeing I had been invited to exercise my spiritual gift by the leadership of the church and was obeying submissively, a gentleman took me to task and dismissed my words with, "Well, God is sovereign, you know. He can even use the wrath of man to praise him." You can imagine that this did not help me to feel confident in my calling.

I talked it over with Angie, who also was busy discovering a real teaching gift. We wondered together why God had gifted us to teach if it was only to teach secular subjects. "It's the 'teaching men' bit, Jill," I remember Angie saying. "Some people think we're not supposed to teach men."

I puzzled over the whole thing. Which men were we not to teach? I wondered. By now we were working five nights a week with teenagers—both men and women. Young teen-aged men and older ones too. We were also working with their parents. When did mini men become maxi men? I mused. When should we stop and hand over so they could teach us?

The whole thing sort of hurt, but I didn't know why. Perhaps it was my "self" nature, I reasoned. Maybe I needed to "die" to this wrong urge to teach the whole wide world about Christ and just settle for half the whole wide world. I wondered about writing instead of speaking, but couldn't see how that would be any different. How could it possibly make a difference if I spoke or wrote the words if men would buy the book? And how would I stop men from picking up my book and reading it if a woman had brought it home?

During some wonderful months when Stuart was home, I poured out my heart to him about the matter. I fully expected him to encourage me to fulfill the expected mission role and do the feminine things—the housework, food, hospitality, and the serving—supportive tasks that had to be done and had always been done by women. After all, I was well acquainted with his home church and my mother-in-law, who made sure I fully understood what she considered the only interpretation of certain obvious Scriptures. Why should I think Stuart would stray far from his roots in his thinking?

To my great surprise, Stuart listened carefully and then said, "Jill, there is no place for your obvious spiritual gifts within the mission program. We would only cause trouble and perhaps division to insist you use your abilities there.

But there's a great big hurting world beyond the mission's walls—go get it!"

And so I did. To my amazement, no one seemed to object to me speaking on street corners, fairgrounds, in drug dives, or anywhere other than the pulpit, on a red carpet, on a Sunday morning. I was not motivated to work the whole theological problem through—that would come later. I simply took my husband's advice, turned my eyes outward, and got busy telling a lost world about a Savior—with the gift that both Stuart and I were coming to recognize had been given to me for that purpose.

As Angie and I worked with the youth program, kids in the area found Christ and became committed Christians. We had our work cut out, coping with all the repercussions. "Whether we should be doing this or not," I said to my friend one day, "there's sure a lot of people outside of Christ who don't seem to know they shouldn't be listening to us."

"Don't let's tell them till they are saved," Angie replied with a grin.

Our days filled up. Now there were few lonely moments. Not that they disappeared altogether. Now and then a huge sense of need for Stuart would engulf me. I would be sitting by our fire in the tiny lodge, the three children fighting for my lap. Clean and warm, sleepy and beautiful David with his big brown eyes, Judy with her clean blonde beauty, and Pete with his daddy's mischievous twinkle would catch my breath. Then the hole in the pit of my stomach would be back and sorrow would fill my heart all over again. Stuart was missing it all. Judy had her hair cut, Pete fell off his bike. The donkey died. Dave played a soccer match, and I was the only mommy without a daddy watching their little boy kick the only goal!

Birthdays came and went. I tried so hard to make the daddy space disappear. That wasn't always easy. I did my best, but many times my best just wasn't good enough. And then my temper would get the better of me. Most times I was angry at myself for not fulfilling my own expectations. I rebuked myself, not only for failing to be a better mom, but for being such a bad "dad" as well. Trying to fill the role of both parents at once became more and more difficult.

Bitterness came calling, and I had a rough period overcoming it. No matter how excited I was with the youth work (and I was excited) or how hard I worked (and I did work hard) or how much I did with the children (schoolwork, skating, walking, reading, supervising playschool in our home), Stuart wasn't there. The future looked pretty bleak. I didn't even want to think about it.

I remember waving him off for one more three-month trip. By then there were very few weeks left at home in a year. Watching the plane soar into the sky with my Stu on board, I began to cry and couldn't stop. I stood there—it felt like forever—with my head against the glass observation deck, sobbing and sobbing. My father had just been diagnosed with incurable cancer, Dave was facing a crucial school entrance exam (it looked as though he might fail), Judy had begun to sleepwalk as soon as her dad left on a trip, and Pete wanted to know why his daddy had to do all the work for Jesus and why some other dads couldn't do some of it! I just couldn't turn around, get back in the car, and face all that responsibility again.

Suddenly I felt a hand on my shoulder. It was a friend, a German man who lodged with Stuart's widowed mother, who had seen me leaning my head on my hands against the window, crying my heart out. He didn't say too much, just offered me a clean hankie to blow my nose, and took me to have a hot English cup of tea. He sat there silently till I got hold of myself, and then he said gently, "It's all right to cry, Jill. God understands. He counts the tears." That was all.

That night, back home with the kids safely in bed, I started the fire and sat by the comforting glow. Turning to my precious Bible, I read, "He puts your tears in a bottle— He writes your tears in his book." I thought about that bottle. I thought about the book. And then I thought about a comment from a friend in similar circumstances—"Jesus left his home for thirty years for us." And I asked God to take away my bitterness, turn it into blessing, and help me one more time. I was sick and tired of being sick and tired! If this was God's plan, I knew he surely couldn't want me to be in this soggy state about it.

The fire burned down, but I put another log on the embers and read on and on and on. I read about Mary of Bethany giving Jesus her little box of ointment—her dowry. It was, in effect, her marriage box, and I told the Lord that night I had discovered some things about myself that I didn't much like. I had not been able to be the Mary I had honestly thought I could be, the good little evangelical wife I had fondly imagined I was. Neither could I break that precious little box over Jesus' feet. But I would do something—I would give him permission to take it.

I don't know when he said thank you and took my very precious little box of ointment, my marriage box. Certainly it was within a few short weeks. I do know I began to see the difference. The aroma of that ointment filled the house. Others sensed it too. There was a fresh fragrant faith in my life that our kids appreciated, Angie observed, the teenagers enjoyed, and above all I knew my husband would be marvelously grateful for.

I sent a long cassette tape to Stuart sharing my experience and telling him I was waiting with more impatience than ever to be together again. I wanted to share this newness with my husband. I knew it didn't mean there would be no more tears (I still cry at airports), and it wouldn't necessarily mean God would change his eternal plan just for me. My husband was, in fact, on the road more, not less, from that time on.

But that crucial prayer, "Lord, make me a Mary," was heard on high, and the bottle in heaven filled with my tears was opened by the angels in order for God to count them all over again and record them in his book of remembrance.

My heart began to sing, and my soul began to dance, and heaven came down and glory filled my soul. It would be all right! For better or for worse we had said—till death, not distance, did us part. That had been the promise—now it must be done. Once again I told the Lord, "As for me and my house, we will serve the Lord."

12

Go West, Young Man—And Take Your Family!

Stuart

Airport reunions had become a regular part of life. Jill would bundle the kids into the car and drive down to Manchester while I was winging home from whatever part of the world I had just visited. They were wonderful, happy times. Except once!

Jill was standing in the crowd outside customs, smiling quietly as David and Peter rushed to meet me with hugs and breathless descriptions of their latest mishaps and assorted adventures. Escaping from their enthusiastic clutches, I embraced Jill, relishing again the warmth of her welcome despite the milling crowds and my clamoring sons. Suddenly I realized Judy was missing.

"Why didn't you bring Judy?" I asked. It seemed as if the crowd around us stopped and looked at me in horror as Jill replied, "This is your daughter, Judy," pointing to a gangly young lady with the brightest of eyes. Judy said nothing, but I saw hurt replace brightness.

Clearly something is wrong when a father does not recognize his own daughter, although it must be said in my defense that she had grown considerably during my absence and her long shoulder-length hair had been cut short. I apologized profusely and made appropriate remarks about how much she had grown and how much I liked her new hairstyle, but it all sounded a trifle hollow, even to me.

Once we were home and the children safely tucked into bed, Jill said, "I think we need to talk." I agreed. "Stu," she said, beginning to cry, "I know this is going to be as hard for you to hear as it will be hard for me to say. But you know I'm totally supportive of your ministry even though it means that you are away from home so much. And you know that we are convinced that if God calls he always equips, but . . . " She hesitated.

"But you are beginning to wonder for how long he has called us to do this kind of work," I interjected.

"Not exactly. I'm wondering if we can sense God's call to something different if we feel the children are suffering."

"They look fine to me," I replied, ever the optimist.

"They are fine as soon as you appear on the scene, but as soon as you leave they are different kids."

"In what way are they different?"

"Did you notice the eczema on David's face? It's related to his nervous disposition. You watch—it will clear up in a day or two now that you are home and reappear as soon as you leave," she explained.

"Couldn't that be coincidence?" I asked hopefully.

"Yes, of course, it could. But there's another coincidence. I haven't wanted to tell you this, but as soon as you leave, Judy sleepwalks into our bedroom each evening, and as soon as you return, she sleeps without disturbance."

"I don't know how to respond," I said, perfectly honest.

"Well, I think your boys are saying that they need a dad, and the unfortunate incident at the airport suggests you need to get to know your daughter."

"I think you're right," I said aloud, thinking to myself, *How on earth can I be home and away at the same time? How can a man be an international evangelist and an active dad to growing children?* I knew there was nothing new about my dilemma. For centuries men and women devoted to both family and ministry had wrestled with the problem and arrived at totally different answers. Some had apparently sacrificed families on the altar of ministry, and others may have offered up their ministry at the shrine of family. Jill and I had no desire to do either.

"There's something else I have to tell you," Jill said after we had sat silently with our thoughts for some time.

"What's that?"

"I don't think I can cope any longer," she blurted out. "And I feel such a failure, and I know that I'm putting you in an impossible situation."

"We're a team, remember?" I said, suddenly realizing that Jill had been bravely carrying an increasing load of responsibility without giving me any indication that she was feeling overwhelmed.

"I can't be Mom and Dad anymore," she summed up her feelings.

"God never expected you to be, and I don't either."

"Then what are we going to do?" she said hesitantly.

"I don't know, but let me tell you what's been happening to me on this trip," I responded, beginning to wonder if there was a connection. Jill relaxed visibly as I began to tell her about a conversation I had had with one of my colleagues with whom I had shared ministry at a pastors' conference. I explained how he had told me after one of my talks, "Stuart, you should realize that your theology incorporates no ecclesiology."

"What did he mean by that?" Jill interrupted, leaping to the defense of her loved one, as is her wont.

"He was showing me that my teaching of spiritual experience is deficient in that it implies that it can be lived in reality. It is to be experienced, enjoyed, and nourished in the community of believers."

"You mean the church?" she asked doubtfully.

"Exactly. And I know that neither of us has had much experience of normal church life for many reasons. But I have been doing a lot of studying on the subject of the local church, and I am convinced the local church is God's method. I would like to be a pastor," I explained, feeling a strange sense of elation as I articulated for the first time thoughts that had been embryonic up until that moment.

"You mean you want to stop traveling and just pastor a church?" Jill asked, trying hard to hide her incredulity.

"No, I'd like to pastor a church that would see the value of my traveling ministry and give me the opportunity to have a home base and an extended outreach," I replied with more enthusiasm than I felt.

"And where d'you think you'll find a church like that?" I heard a voice saying, and with a start I recognized Jill's voice asking aloud what I had been querying in silence.

"I don't know, but if God is in this, there'll be one somewhere and we'll find it," I replied with confidence.

"Stu, the thought of being together as a family, having a ministry together, and being part of a church family is so exciting that I hardly dare think about it."

"Me neither, but let's explore the possibilities and see what turns up in God's plan," I said even as a troubling thought hit me. Could we really leave the work at Capernwray and our friends, colleagues, and mentors of many years? Could we leave the lovely home we and the Capernwray staff had built with our own hands? Could we walk away from the delightful pastoral scene I could see through the French windows? Rolling grassland, grazing sheep, highland cattle with handlebar horns, flowering chestnuts, sycamores, acres of burgeoning pine plantation, and banks of purple, pink, and white rhododendron? And the kids from all over Europe? Could we walk away from them and the local kids who were like extended family? I began to have my doubts, but I kept them to myself.

By the time I left for the U.S.A. a few weeks later, Jill had succumbed to migraine headaches and an ulcer—and I had no further doubts. Her health was showing signs of wear and tear, and my interests were beginning to change. I was beginning to realize that my "little children," who Jill was such an expert at caring for, were no longer little children and they needed me. To my surprise, I found that if I allowed myself to think about it (which I had for years carefully avoided doing to any great extent), I needed them, too.

Jill had occasionally mentioned to me that I seemed self-contained and apparently perfectly capable of managing just fine without the family. This had bothered me because I recognized that there was an element of truth in it. *Of necessity,* I had reasoned to myself, *I must not allow myself to be lonely or to think about missing the family because the Lord has called me to be away from them, and, therefore, to dwell on such thoughts would be nonproductive and could well become counterproductive.*

Secretly I occasionally wondered if I might be so good at controlling my feelings that I might finish up an unfeeling person. But not being given to a great deal of introspection, I simply got on with the job at hand, rejoicing that in some small measure I was experiencing something that Dietrich Bonhoeffer had called "The Cost of Discipleship."

My interest in pastoring continued to grow as I studied the biblical view of the church. I was intrigued with the thought of staying with a group of people over a period of time and helping them work out the things I was preaching. In itinerant ministry I rarely stayed anywhere longer than one week, so I could preach with great fervor and authority without having the somewhat uncomfortable experience of staying around to see if the theory I propounded actually worked. Often when people asked me practical questions relating to what I had been saying I would respond, "Well, that's really outside my area of expertise. You should talk to your pastor about that." I began to wonder what the pastor would say if I were the pastor!

Then I thought of my own children moving toward adolescence. For years I had been working with other people's teenagers, and I liked the idea of being involved with my own. But there was still the nagging doubt about whether a church like the one I had envisioned existed, and if it did, would they be interested in someone who had never studied to be a pastor?

These questions and many more were soon to be answered. For many years I had known a lanky, vibrant Texan preacher by the name of Bob Hobson. We had often shared ministry, and I knew that he had a singularly effective ministry in a church in the greater Milwaukee area. One fine day I flew into Milwaukee at Bob's invitation to conduct a series of meetings at Elmbrook Church. As I came up the escalator in the arrival concourse, I saw Bob standing at the top. He shouted to me, "I'm announcing my resignation tomorrow, and I'm joining you on the Capern-wray staff."

"Don't announce it tomorrow. They'll never hear a word I say all week," I shouted back. "Tell them next Sunday after I've left."

"Okay," he replied amiably, "as long as you help me find a replacement." So I did: me!

Actually it wasn't quite that simple. As I ministered at Elmbrook that week, I quickly recognized that the church was relatively young and spiritually alive. Many of the people were new believers, and they were bringing their friends and relatives to the various events. The church itself had not developed many traditions, mainly because those attending came from widely different traditions or no tradition at all. The one thing they had in common was an excitement about the Lord Jesus in both knowing him and in making him known. I liked what I saw.

Halfway through the week, as Bob and I and one of the church leaders, Willie Treu, were eating lunch, Bob asked, "Well, have you thought of a pastor for us?"

"How about me? Would I do?" I replied only semi-facetiously.

"I knew as soon as I saw you that you would be our next pastor," said Willie.

"What else d'you know about me that I'm not aware of?" I asked with a laugh.

"Nothing! But you'll come, just you see!" he said confidently.

Before the week was through I had talked with the deacons and by phone with Jill and, incredibly, it seemed that everything was going to fit perfectly. They wanted a pastor, I wanted to pastor; I wanted freedom to minister outside the church's four walls, they thought that was a great idea; I told them I had never been a pastor, they said they had only just become a church; I said that I would not be doing all the work, they said they wanted to be involved; I said our family needed time to get to know each other, they said they would be delighted to help.

We waited to make a final decision until I returned home to England. When I did, I found Jill and the children filled with anticipation. But understandably, our widowed mothers were not as enthusiastic, although they both recognized that we had our own lives to live. Our emotions were torn at this point because both of us were anxious to care for those who in earlier days had cared for us. However, Jill had a sister, Shirley, who lived close to their mother, and I had a brother, Bernard, living close to my mother. We talked those matters through as families and were given the green light.

Leaving Capernwray and all that it meant to us was no easy matter either. But we decided that although continuing ministry there would be profitable, it would not afford the family and pastoral experiences we were convinced were necessary for us at that stage of our lives. So we "bit the bullet" after much thought, counsel, and prayer—and sensing that God was opening a door in the West for us, we announced we were going!

Reactions were mixed. One British evangelical leader introduced us at a large meeting as the "ones who left the sinking ship." Others hinted darkly that we were going because of the money to be made in America. Some friends congratulated me on discovering a wife and family at last, while an evangelist friend tried to warn us away from Milwaukee, telling us that Dwight L. Moody had called it the graveyard of evangelists. Another friend called to say, "Do you realize that Milwaukee is the largest city in the U.S.A. to which Billy Graham has never been invited?"

Meanwhile the Elmbrook congregation voted to extend a call to us—with but one negative vote. Jill was naturally most anxious to discover the identity of the sole dissenter, so she asked the chairman of the board, as soon as she met him, if he had any idea who it was.

"Oh yes," he said with a grin.

"How do you know?" she responded. "I thought it was a secret ballot."

"It was," he replied. "But when I announced the results, one of the men turned and glared at his wife, and she turned bright red!" Knowing the couple, the chairman had guessed that the husband had told his wife to vote nay and she had failed to do so, apparently assuming there would be others doing the same and that her defection from the ranks of dissenters would never be noticed. I know the said couple's identity, but I never told Jill!

▄▄▄▄▄▄

Everything was moving ahead beautifully, and then we hit a snag. The United States Naturalization and Immigration Service had a priority entry procedure for ministers, and so we assumed that our visa would come through in a matter of a few weeks. Unfortunately, I did not possess a certificate of ordination to prove I was a minister, so my visa was denied. I appealed and was told that if I was a bonafide minister, I would have certification. A number of internationally recognized ministry friends wrote letters assuring the people at the American embassy that I was genuine. Finally they relented and said the visa would be forthcoming.

Instead I got a phone call weeks later, saying that I had written books and therefore was an author and not a minister. A further visit was needed to explain that it is customary for ministers to write sermons, and twelve or thirteen of them, when put together, form a book. "The visa will be forthcoming," I was assured. But another phone call, weeks later, raised another issue. "We see that you have been behind the Iron Curtain. We need to talk about your reasons for having contact with Communist regimes!"

"I was visiting believers in the churches over there," I explained.

"You're not allowed to preach. What were you really doing?" they inquired skeptically.

"You're right, technically, but over there they ask you to 'bring greetings' for about forty-five minutes to an hour, and then the pastor gives a five-minute sermon," I assured them.

Eventually they concluded I was not a closet Communist who posed a threat to the security of the United States, and promised the visa would be forthcoming. Instead, another phone call raised the issue of my having associated with people with criminal records, the drug scene, and other disreputable segments of society. I pointed out that Jesus had done similar things and wondered aloud if he would have been granted a visa. That seemed to help, and again the visa was promised.

In the interim a friend of mine, the late Hal Brooks, pastor of North Richland Hills Baptist Church in Fort Worth, Texas, had called. "Stuart," he said, "we all know you have devoted yourself to full-time ministry for the last eleven or twelve years, but because you were in itinerant rather than pastoral ministry, you never had a local church ordain you. We at North Richland Hills would count it a privilege to confirm your existing call and certify it." So that is what we did.

The next time the American embassy representatives called, I said I would travel to London to talk to them. I was told it was uncertain that I would be granted an interview, but I went and eventually sat down with someone important. To my amazement he said, "Mr. Briscoe, according to our definition you are not a minister, and therefore, your application is denied."

"With all due respect, sir, according to your definition Billy Graham is not a minister of the gospel. Your definition of a minister of the gospel is actually a definition of a pastor of a local church, but the Scripture and the church recognize that there are ministers who specialize in teaching, evangelism, and prophecy. I fit into those categories."

"It's all very difficult, Mr. Briscoe," he said, shuffling the papers in my file. "If only you had a certificate, there would be no problem."

"But I do," I responded triumphantly, producing my new certificate of ordination.

"You do?" he questioned, peering at the piece of paper as if to determine it was a forgery. Apparently satisfied, he smiled and said, "That's wonderful, I'll see to the paperwork immediately!" And he did.

Meanwhile back at Elmbrook another cloud had risen on the horizon. Unknown to us, some of the congregation had begun to wonder aloud if the delay in getting a visa was actually God's saying that I was not the man of the hour, and an effort was put forward to rescind the call that the church had extended. Some of the people insisted that the call should stand and they all should get on their knees. Unfortunately, opinions were divided, feelings were hurt, and, as is often the case, factions developed. The leaders of the church decided not to tell us anything about these developments, but we were to discover them all too soon, once we arrived.

It was necessary for us to visit the American embassy in London in person to receive our visas, and as the children had never seen the capital city of their homeland, which they were about to leave, we decided to take them with us. As we showed them the sights and explained the history of their country, I had fleeting feelings of unease. I was going to uproot my family from the only family history and societal structure they knew and transplant them into a culture that, while similar, was still foreign to them.

How foreign, we soon realized. The kids were anxious to know what they would be required to do at the embassy. Jokingly I told them they would have to answer questions about America.

"Like what?" asked Judy, always the first to speak.

"Oh, like, Who is the president of the United States?" I replied.

"That's easy," said Judy.

"Okay, who is he?" David asked.

"Dick Van Dyke," she replied with great confidence.

"No, it isn't," said Pete. "It's Tom 'n Jerry!"

Once again laughter came to the rescue. We tried to rectify the misconceptions and traveled home clutching the visas that, by this time, had cost us a year of our lives.

The sixteenth of November 1970 was a cold, foggy day with downpours of rain. We were packed up early in the morning to leave for Manchester Airport and the new world. But first there were many sad farewells at Capernwray, when customary British reserve cracked more than once. It was almost exactly twenty-three years since I had first visited Capernwray, and much of my spiritual growth was directly related to that place and many of the people who now bade us good-bye. We took a last look at our cedarwood home, then the lodge, the pastureland, and the country lanes, got on the freeway we had driven a thousand times, and finally arrived at the airport. To our surprise, many of our Manchester and Liverpool friends and Jill's sister, Shirley, were awaiting us there.

In addition to the five of us and ten suitcases, we were taking with us our magnificent golden retriever, "Gold Link of Green Glen"—or Prince as he was known to all and sundry who were aware of his endearing and wayward habits. I had been instructed to sedate him, so fortunately he was suitably mellow as we arrived in the crowded airport. As soon as I got to the desk and started to check the bags I noticed a traveling box of the kind used to transport dogs.

"That's your box, Mr. Briscoe," said the clerk, noting my glance.

"No, that's not big enough."

"It's the one you ordered," he responded firmly.

"Why would I order a box that size for a dog this size?" I queried equally firmly.

"It'll have to do. It's the one we've provided," he asserted more firmly.

"Absolutely not," I replied. "It would be inhumane even if he would fit."

"What seems to be the problem?" asked the supervisor.

Nothing *seemed* to be the problem. The wrong size box *was* the problem. By this time the flight had been called, so I urged Jill to board with the children.

"Don't let them go without you," Jill said desperately.

"And don't come without Prince," added David helpfully.

After much negotiation the correct box was found, a very sleepy Prince was put in it, and I boarded the plane to be met by rows and rows of sullen looks. "Judy just announced to the plane that the delay was because of our dog," Jill whispered.

No sooner had I sat down than a cabin attendant came to me and said, "You will have to disembark, Mr. Briscoe. We can't get the dog's box in the hold."

"I can't possibly disembark. My family and I are emigrating. Bring the dog up here; he's practically unconscious!"

"It's against the rules. You'll just have to get off the plane and fly with your dog later."

"I'm sorry to be difficult, but that is quite out of the question." He left, returning a few minutes later and whispering confidentially in my ear, "Follow me, Mr. Briscoe."

"I'm not going anywhere!"

"Please, I'll explain," he added with a touch of desperation.

"Dad's leaving us to go to America on our own," wailed Judy.

"The captain says you can fly with the dog in the cockpit but nobody must see you," he explained. "But you'll have to get the dog. The handlers are afraid of him." I ran down the steps in the pouring rain to where the box stood with Prince inside.

"Looks like a ruddy lion to me," said one handler.

"Wouldn't get me to open that box for a hundred pounds," added another. Prince had never looked less fearsome in his life. In fact, I carried him over my shoulder up the steps, all the time trying to look invisible as instructed.

On arriving in the cockpit with my load of retriever, soaked to the skin, I was greeted by the captain, who said amiably, "Nice dog you've got there. I have three retrievers, two donkeys, a peacock, and a wife at home." With that we set off. Prince and me in the cockpit, Jill and the kids in the cabin wondering where we were. Prince slept until we landed in London. As we approached the gate he leapt up without warning, put his front paws on top of the instrument panel, and peered out of the window between the captain and first officer. The mechanic directing the plane to the gate suddenly realized something like a lion was staring at him from the cockpit of a Comet airliner. One could imagine from the look on his face that he thought that he was hallucinating and probably vowing never to touch another drop as long as he lived!

I thanked the captain profusely. "Don't mention it," he responded. "And if you ever tell anyone, I'll deny it," he added with a wink. With that he left the cockpit, then turned back and said, "Better not let anybody see you take the dog off the plane." Not having any idea how to accomplish that feat, having never practiced it before, I decided to walk out among the crowd, hoping Prince, who was by this time showing some of his natural ebullience, would be lost in the crowd. No such luck!

"Ooh, look Mom, that poor man's blind, he's got a guide dog," shouted a small girl pointing in my direction.

"Ssh, don't point—it's rude," said her mother as I tried to look slightly disabled, not having practiced that either.

"That's the way to stop them 'ijackers," spoke up an elderly gentleman with a military air and moustache to match. I quickly switched from being disabled to looking slightly mysterious and threatening, all the time keeping an eye open for potential "hijackers." This I had never practiced before either.

Once inside the terminal Prince decided he liked unconscious better than conscious. His legs splayed out pointing north, south, east, and west, and nothing I could do changed his posture. So I just pulled on his lead and he slid along on the polished floor quite happily.

Needless to say, Prince and I had a happy reunion with the family. Then I remembered we had no box for Prince and we had paid a lot of money for the one last seen in the

Manchester rain. I called the appropriate department, who informed me either (1) I was not in London; (2) if I was in London I couldn't possibly have the dog with me; and (3) if I insisted I was in London with my dog I must have my box, and did I think they were so stupid that they couldn't see through my scheme to get another box for free? Further negotiations resulted in my forking out for another box.

By this time we were in dire danger of missing the flight to Chicago. For this reason London Airport was treated to one of its most unusual PA announcements ever: "Will the family trying to fly their dog to Chicago please get on board the plane."

"That's Prince they're talking about," announced Judy to the watching crowds. Prince was finally em-boxed, we were em-planed, and as we recounted the latest saga of Prince, we laughed till we cried, till we fell silent thinking our own thoughts. I was sure God had said, "Go West, young man—and take your family (and dog) with you."

13

Home Is the Will of God

*P*rince shot out of his cage like a bolt from the blue, clinging like a limpet to the end of his leash. Dave was carried along by the momentum of his heaving shoulders. They slid across the shiny marble immigration area together, slipping and sliding, the retriever's eyes wild as he pointed his nose toward what looked to him like a neat, inviting, shiny tree. Fortunately, David discerned his intent and diverted him around the silver pole in the lobby of the airport toward the exit!

Poor Prince had been shut up for far too many hours in his cage—sleeping off the effects of the drugs he had been given. But now he was up and ready to go and discover America, all by himself if need be. He was greeted warmly by loving pats, friendly faces, and excited chatter.

"Look, Mum," Pete chirped, "the taxis are yellow, and someone's written all over them!" Gone were the black London cabs with their snub noses and the doubledecker London buses. Gone the bright brass letterboxes smiling smugly from the front doors of the tiny, tidy rows of houses that embroidered our English streets. Now our letters would find their home in funny gray cylinders stuck on top of sticks. Now we were in the new world: It was the seventies, and this was Chicago. "Is this where Al Capone lives?" inquired Dave excitedly.

We loaded our baggage (not luggage) into the trunk (not the boot) of the waiting automobile (not car) and were soon flying along the highways (not motorways) past blocks of apartments (not flats). Gone were the cheerful friendly English bobbies—named after "Robert" Peel, who created the English police force—with their tall, round helmets, notebooks, and rubber truncheons. Now we were protected by the American cop, flat-hatted, with rather frightening armaments in his belt.

"Why do they carry guns?" asked Judy, wide-eyed and rather scared.

"I told you," David replied impatiently, "in case they meet Al Capone!"

Gone my English roses, misted wet cobblestones, the emerald grass. I couldn't help it, but Blake's lines—"England's green and pleasant land"—popped into my head. I was missing it already.

But now "this America" beckoned, and the excitement of the moment chased my momentary nostalgia away. God had brought us here, and he would help us to adjust, I told myself.

A sudden vibration under the wheels of the van made Judy giggle. "That feels funny, Mummy," she said. The road ruts were slowing us down for the first toll booth.

"Judy, do you want to throw the money in the basket?" Willie Treu, our new friend, asked her.

"Oh, yes please," our daughter responded eagerly.

"What are we paying for?" David asked with interest.

"The road," Willie replied, grinning.

I don't know what this piece of information did for Judy, but somehow the little booth with the tired, dispirited woman manning it reminded me of the reason for coming. People were the same everywhere. The lady looked frazzled, ready for a good night's sleep. Where did she live, and what was she going home to? I wondered. Suddenly I felt quiet inside. In the years ahead I would meet lots of ladies like this one. God could make the difference—I knew he could, and I wanted her to know it, too.

At last we were "home"—entering the village of Brookfield, outside Milwaukee, Wisconsin, home of the Bucks, the Brewers, and the beer that made Milwaukee famous. Prince was ecstatic. Before I could prevent it, David had released him and he was gone! It was sort of a prophetic moment—for the next fourteen years we would be chasing him round the neighborhood when he "escaped" from us. He was used to vast acres of English countryside with dozens of sheep and cows to chase.

Now, at the age of two, he would have to learn to be a proper American dog—doing what he was told to do. Looking back, I realize he must have made a very definite doggy decision that first night never to become a proper American dog—and he never did! About an hour later, he turned up, wagging his tail, with someone's doormat hanging out of the corner of his mouth (he was a retriever). We dispatched Dave to find out the mat's owner and set about discovering our lovely new home.

The church had done a masterful job providing everything we needed. The house was beautiful. I must confess I had a little heart twinge, feeling the need for a sight or feel of something familiar, something worn or dear, but we had agreed to sell everything. It didn't matter, I told myself sternly, that everything had been chosen for us—after all, the choices were choice!

The adjustments were sweet, funny, shocking, and unexpected. It wasn't just the difference in the American and

English accents; it was the phrases and actual words. We found out lorries were trucks, pavements were sidewalks, and when I wanted to tell the kids to "pull their socks up," I needed to say instead, "Get it all together."

"We don't have to be polite anymore," Judy announced cheerily, coming in from school and plunking her lunch box (no satchels anymore) on the countertop. I had thought that school was school everywhere, but there were schools and then there were schools, I discovered. The school where Judy didn't need to be polite anymore (and to her added delight could wear her own clothes, not her little navy blue school uniform) had six hundred kids (not children). She had been used to sixty in a two-room schoolhouse over at Kellet on the Green near Capernwray.

The whole country stopped for Thanksgiving while we blandly went right on with life—arriving at the office and sending the kids to school. The new vacations really threw us off. I learned that first year to realize a vacation day had arrived if there was no mail (not post) in the box. I felt really funny, too, when no one celebrated our holidays (vacations): Boxing Day, Whitsuntide, and August Bank holiday went by without anyone missing a step. After thirty-five years of celebrating them, I felt sort of unpatriotic when no one noticed.

"I say, old chap, shall we have a spot of tea," a young, yet very English voice said when I picked up the phone one day. It was Pete! I burst into tears. "He's teasing us about our English accent," I wept on my husband's shoulder. Stuart laughed, thinking that was extremely funny, but I began to see that my adjustments were showing. Of course, people had their own adjustments to make to us, too.

Stuart and I teased each other unmercifully most of the time. Living in Britain, where people seldom complimented one another, couples engaged in friendly banter, which can be almost a "love language." In fact, I usually knew something was amiss if Stuart stopped teasing me. Imagine our surprise, therefore, when a concerned deacon from our new church visited us to make sure all was well with our marriage! I was bewildered.

"How do we behave in public, then?" I asked Stuart after we had put the deacon's mind at ease and he had gone home.

"Just as we've always behaved," Stuart answered cheerfully. "They'll catch on soon enough. Anyway, I think people tend to take themselves a mite too seriously over here. So maybe we can help them to loosen up a bit!"

I was to discover we were "on show," watched with interest all the time. I hadn't bargained on my reaction to that. "I have absolutely no idea why the washing powder (not detergent) we use to do the washing (not the laundry) at the store (shop) we shop at, or the clothes we wear, should be of any interest whatsoever to our 'church world' in general and to a few in particular," I complained, "but apparently they are!"

"That's how it is over here," Stuart answered, "but it can work to our advantage. You'll find people will openly share their personal lives with us as well." He was right.

Now I really suffered culture shock. I struggled to know what to do with the extraordinary personal revelations that were spilled out to me, a total stranger. In fact, twenty years later I still marvel at this. The English reserve that still has me addressing colleagues we worked with for twelve years as Mr. or Mrs. reminds me that habits die hard. To bare one's soul at such a depth and seemingly at the drop of a hat was at first an acute embarrassment to me until I saw the obvious opportunity for ministry. Then I saw what Stuart was trying to say.

"Stuart," I gasped after one of the most bizarre telephone conversations I had ever had, "everyone talks about their hysterectomies as if they've just been to the dentist. I can't remember ever having heard anyone even mention the word back home!"

Stuart ignored the matter of the hysterectomy and asked me gently, "Home—where's home, Jill?"

"Here," I replied hesitantly.

"Here," he replied firmly.

I had once heard someone say, "Home is the will of God," and I knew the truth of that. There was absolutely no doubt in my mind that we were exactly where the Lord wanted us to be. It was just a matter of my heart catching up with my faith.

"Home is where you and the children are," I affirmed. "Home is where David reads a book and Judy rearranges her dolls and Pete bounces a ball. Home is all of us under the same roof, together at last. All of us teasing and touching, laughing and loving, and actually having our feet under the same table all at the same time."

Just before we moved a continent away, David and I had been getting on each other's nerves. One day after we were in our new routine, I suddenly realized my son and I were having fun together. The pressures were off me. "There's a huge difference now that you're here for David," I told my husband. "Now there's a daddy in the daddy space. That little boy is one happy mite (sorry, camper!)." What a help it was to have another adult to say no when it had to be said, yes when a risk needed taking, and maybe when time was needed to weigh the options. Now I could relax with David and let Stuart play the heavy when necessary. It was time for David and me to build instead of battle over our mother-son relationship. We could breathe again. How I thanked God for that!

Meanwhile, at Elmbrook we had been given a terrific welcome. Despite some problems, we were off and running. The time came for our first church meeting, and naively I said to Stuart, "I'm so excited. They're going to talk about changing some things in the constitution, aren't they?"

"Yes," he said, "it will be interesting." And it most certainly was.

I sat by a long-standing member of the church, who began to get extremely agitated as the debate got under way. He began making derogatory comments to me out of the side of his mouth about the proponents of the proposals and the leaders of the church, my husband included. *What does he expect me to do,* I wondered in amazement—*agree with him? He knows very well who I am!* My husband sat there calmly, and the hotter it got the cooler he became. He put in a word here and there but didn't defend himself or the leaders. (He wanted to make sure everyone had his or her say, he explained later.)

Well, the man next to me had his say all right. In the most confidential manner he began to say all sorts of personal and not very complimentary things about Stuart. I glared at him (which didn't make any difference at all), and when I couldn't stand it any longer, I said, "Really, he's a relative of mine you know!" He stopped, looking surprised, as if he couldn't understand my reaction. This was my chance. It didn't appear that Stuart had any intention of defending himself, I thought, and so I jumped up saying resolutely to myself, *This is what partnership is all about! Yes, this is what wives are for.* I hadn't a clue as to the issues in question. I was just horrified at the tone of the meeting. I couldn't believe the anger in the voices, the tears, the upset people. Was this the church Jesus Christ had died for?

"I'd like to say—" I began. Don't ask me what I would have liked to say because I don't remember, and I didn't say it for very long. After a few words I burst dramatically into floods of tears—and burst even more dramatically out of the sanctuary and into the ladies' room, where I decided to die! It didn't help me to hear Stuart saying, as I departed, "Thank you, Jill, for your contribution."

A dear lady, Win, ran after me, helped me wash my face, listened to my lament most sympathetically, and then gently but firmly insisted that we go back into the sanctuary together.

"I can't," I wailed. "Here I am, the pastor's wife, making a total fool of myself!"

"You must get on the bicycle, Jill," said Win. "People who fall off their bicycle must get right back on, or they will never learn to ride."

"I don't want to ride this particular bicycle. I want to go home!"

"Well," she replied lovingly but firmly, "you can't. God sent you to us, and until he sends you somewhere else as clearly as he sent you here, you'd better settle yourself. We love you and Stuart, and this will pass. You'll see."

Could there possibly be another Joan Thomas this side of the Atlantic? I wondered. How could I be that lucky? Another wise woman to tell me to "have a good cry, wash my face, get up and get on with it"? Sniffling into my tissues (not hankies), I allowed her argument to prevail and followed her meekly back into the sanctuary. The church was praying. Thankfully, I hurriedly bowed my head and kept going until the "Amen" was long over and only Stuart was left.

"Well," I mumbled, "sorry about that. I'll do better next time." He gave me a wry smile, kissed me, and said he thought I'd done just fine. *Good,* I thought, *then any improvement will obviously be much appreciated!*

I learned that day that a pastor's wife has to learn to handle criticism. Not necessarily criticism about herself (I think I'd had that licked for years)—but criticism of her husband. Criticism from strangers and from friends, criticism from fans and enemies alike. From the aged and the young. From people who know a lot and from people who know nothing at all. The thing that hurt most was the unfairness of it all. How could people say the awful things they had said when my husband was putting out so much for them? How could they suspect his motives when I knew he was trying his level best to do the right thing?

That thought gave me a clue. If I knew these things about my husband, then surely God knew all about them too. Finding great comfort in 1 Corinthians 4:1-5, I prayed that Stuart would be able to say with Paul that it is a very small thing that I am judged of you. I noticed Paul didn't say, "It's not anything at all," because he knew we need to "own" what we deserve when we are criticized, but I was also reminded that Christ can help it to be a small thing and not the end of the world.

"This is different," I said to Stuart late that night. "I've never been shot at from the inside before."

"We just need to keep our perspective," he replied. "We are just beginning. It will probably get worse before it gets better."

How could it get worse? I thought. I didn't have long to wait to find out. If I thought it was tough when my husband was criticized, that was nothing compared to the kids coming under fire. That wasn't fair either!

On a Sunday, having waited all week to see me, people would demand my total attention, and then I'd hear them talking about all the things our kids got into while I was tied up, talking to them about their kids. I was used to community living, but this was different again, another sort of challenge. I tried to take it in stride. Ignoring "the gallery," I tried to discipline the children as usual—as if there were no one there. It was hard—until I stopped trying to play the perfect Christian mother and instead let myself be the normal imperfect one I was!

Soon after we had settled in, Stuart's mother headed over the Atlantic in our direction. This was pretty brave of her, since she didn't drive a car and hadn't ever been on a plane in her life, but Mary had never been lacking in courage. A little apprehensive, I wondered how we would get along together for three long months, and that with an interested congregation watching.

Reading the book of Ruth, I reflected how like Naomi and Orpah's relationship Mother's and mine had been. Naomi and Orpah had a "nothing much" sort of relationship. Nothing like the one that existed between Ruth and her mother-in-law. Coming to a crossroads, Orpah kissed Naomi and went her own way. Ruth, on the other hand, clung to Naomi and committed herself unreservedly to her for the rest of her life.

Why the story struck me I didn't know—until a short time into the visit when Mother discovered one more of the cancers that had dogged her for too many years. Now Ruth chapter 1 leapt from the pages to challenge me, especially verse 17: "Where you die I will die, and there I will be buried. May the LORD deal with me, be it ever so severely, if anything but death separates you and me." How could I become a Ruth so instantly? I asked myself. When you've been content with a "nothing much" relationship, it's hard to grow self-giving love overnight.

I struggled hard with it. I didn't want her to suffer and die here. Not in front of the kids. What would we do about the nursing, and the money for the bills (she had no insurance to cover her in the U.S.A.)? I knew I needed to be a Ruth, but in all honesty I didn't want to be. I didn't feel good about feeling like this and yet couldn't seem to do anything about it. To make matters worse, I couldn't even tell Stuart. What would I say—"I want your mother to go back to England"? How hurt he would be. I shared my struggle with our doctor. He praised me for being honest. But being honest didn't exempt me from being what I should be.

I was forced to face some facts that hadn't even entered into my thinking when we had sold everything we owned and emigrated to the States. The care of our widowed mothers! I thought of my own sweet Peggy and my tummy did little somersaults. I pushed the possibility of her ever dying far away from me and attended to the problem at hand. I began to ask God to radically change my attitude toward my mother-in-law. "Please don't ever let her know I don't want her to stay," I begged the Lord—and then, "O Lord, I'm so ashamed that this is the best I can do." *Is it realistic to expect to love other people's relatives as much as your own?* I worried. But this was Stuart's mom, not just anybody's relative. That was a starting place. I could love and care for her because I loved and cared for him. I could start by doing it for Stuart, and hopefully I would end up doing it for her!

She had, after all, given him birth and brought him to Christ. A rush of thankfulness swept over me. I'd tell her how thankful I was for these things, I decided. Ruth had verbalized her concern for Naomi, and so I verbalized my concern too, and even managed to tell Mom Briscoe we wanted her to stay till the end so we could look after her. Like Ruth, I discovered in the months ahead that I needed to be "steadfastly determined to go with her" and let my feelings do what they would.

We adjusted. We moved to accommodate the nursing, and we prepared the children as best we knew how. We altered our schedules, rolled up our sleeves, took a deep breath, and prepared to do battle. And what a battle it was. Mother toughed it out. She shed few tears. "What's the good of crying—that doesn't help," she announced resolutely as she suffered three grueling months of chemotherapy. A rugged determination to suffer well to the glory of God and a firm faith in the Lord she loved saw her through. Stuart's presence was a huge encouragement to her, and I became increasingly thankful she had stayed. She taught us all how to die, and you don't get too many real-life seminars quite like that.

People were so good to us. Our new American friends came through. Doctors donated their services, nurses from the church gave their time, and our love, admiration, and appreciation blossomed and grew for this mighty lady of faith and fortitude.

And then after a doctor's appointment in which the worst-case scenario was presented to us, Mother decided to go home! There was no changing her mind. By now we were beginning to enjoy a Naomi-and-Ruth relationship. God had worked a miracle in our hearts. But she wanted to die in England and be buried by her beloved Stanley.

"It's foolish; there's no one at home to look after you," Stuart protested.

"No matter. I'm going," she announced in a way that brooked no argument.

Waving her off at the airport, I glanced at Stuart's face. I think we both knew it was the last time we would see her this side of glory. I took his hand, and we went home in a deep silence.

The Lord looked after his brave little lady as we dared to believe he would. Stuart's brother Bernard, also in full-time itinerant work, had a three-month trip to New Zealand canceled at the very last minute. God's clocks keep perfect time. Bernard brought his mother home from the hospital, moved into her little bungalow, and nursed her to the end. The circle was completed. She who had given Bernard birth and cradled him in her arms now lay helplessly dependent in his arms, as she met the Lord she had loved and served so faithfully for over fifty years.

Now we had buried three of our parents. Only Peggy, my beloved mom, was left—and she was three thousand miles away! Once again I felt as though I was torn in two. What would I do when her turn came? I began to panic. It was only as I buried myself in the Word that peace and comfort came. Hadn't the Lord looked after Mom Briscoe? Wouldn't he do the same for Peggy?

It was so hard thinking of others caring for her—strangers in a nursing home perhaps. I knew Shirley, my sister, was there for her, and two women closer than my mother and sister were hard to imagine. But would I have a part? I think my greatest tussle with homesickness hit me then. Reading the account of Christ on the cross, I realized how hard it must have been for him to give his mother into John's care, even as much as he loved that special disciple. He had come to fulfill God's plan for his life, and his hands were tied, or, more accurately, pinned into place with a hammer and nails. *The emotional wounds Christ suffered were far deeper than even the terrible physical scars,* I thought.

We had done the right thing, Stuart assured me when I shared my apprehensions about my own mother with him. "God called us to America. Remember what the Lord told the Hudson Taylors when, far away in the interior of

China, they were desperately worried about their children shut up in an internment camp during the Japanese-Chinese conflict. God had spoken to Mrs. Taylor clearly saying, 'You look after the things that are precious to me, and I'll look after the things that are precious to you!' "

I tried to rest in that. That night, thinking of this particularly tough aspect of Christian service, I read Amy Carmichael's piercing meditation . . .

Hast thou no scar?
No hidden scar on foot, or side, or hand?
I hear thee sung as mighty in the land
I hear them hail thy bright ascendant star,
Hast thou no scar?

Hast thou no wound?
Yet I was wounded by the archers, spent,
Leaned Me against a tree to die; and rent
By ravening beasts that compassed Me,
  I swooned:
Hast thou no wound?

No wound? no scar?
Yet, as the Master shall the servant be,
And pierced are the feet that follow Me;
But thine are whole: can he have followed far
Who has nor wound nor scar?

Amy Carmichael, *Toward Jerusalem* (Fort Washington, Penn.: Christian Literature Crusade, 1977)

I fell asleep. The matter was settled for a little while.

14

Adjustments

Stuart

As I had spent quite a lot of time ministering in the States, I felt I had a pretty good idea of what America and Americans were like. So I didn't expect to have to make too many adjustments. I knew, of course, that I would have to adjust to being a pastor and a full-time father, but there was nothing I wanted to do more. On the other hand, Jill had spent very little time in the U.S.A., and the children, none at all.

On arrival we had decided to give the children a week to adjust, but after two or three days they announced they were bored and asked if they could please go to school. This they promptly did and discovered to their surprise that they were regarded as minor celebrities. They had no idea what people meant when they said, "We just love your cute accents." As far as they knew they were simply speaking English! This did not prevent Peter from acquiring an authentic Midwest American accent within the first week in our new home. I told the kids that it was perfectly appropriate for them to develop American accents but it would not be appropriate for them to adopt some of the sloppy grammar of their newfound friends. The confusion of adverbs and adjectives seemed to cause particular problems—and still does occasionally to this day.

To our surprise, the first scholastic adjustment problem came from Judy. She announced at the end of the first week that she did not like school and did not intend to return.

"Why?" I inquired with some degree of alarm.

"Because all week the teacher has been telling us stories about the Patriots and the Redcoats."

"Uh, huh," I encouraged her. "Go on!"

"Well, the teacher said the Patriots were the good people and the Redcoats were bad people."

"So?"

"Well, today she said the Redcoats who were the bad people were English, and the Patriots who were the good people were Americans."

"Oh, I see the problem," I sympathized.

"Dad, we're English, and we're not bad people. Why does she say that Americans are good and English are bad?" she asked indignantly.

"She didn't say that all English are bad and all Americans are good. She was teaching you the story of the War of Independence when the Americans fought the English," I explained patiently.

"But why were the English bad because they fought Americans?" she demanded.

"Honey," I said, taking my nine-year-old bundle of feminine indignation on my knee, "you have to realize there are two sides to every story and she got hold of the wrong one!" I could see that being around the kids as they asked their questions, faced their doubts, and fought their battles was going to be a challenge and a privilege.

Jill had her problems, too. One day I answered the phone and a lady I knew said, "Oh, Stuart, I just called to invite Jill to a shower. Do you think she would like to come with me?" Knowing what she meant, and knowing that Jill would not know, I could not resist the temptation (to be honest, I didn't try) to say, "She's right here; you have a word with her." Jill took the phone and, on hearing the invitation, a look of horror came over her face. Putting her hand over the mouthpiece she said, "There's a weird woman who wants me to go to the shower with her!"

"Well," I replied, struggling to keep a straight face, "that's what Americans do. When in Rome do as the Romans, Jill."

"But . . . " she expostulated.

The lady on the phone, aware of Jill's hesitation, interrupted helpfully, "Oh, Jill, please don't be shy. There'll be at least twenty-three other women there!"

Explanation time having arrived, I intervened, and Jill agreed to go with her natural modesty intact. "Churchill was right," I said cheerfully, "the British and the Americans are two people divided by a common language."

"Very funny," said Jill, sounding rather like Queen Victoria, who was not amused.

※※※※※

Not everything was amusing in those early days. A couple of weeks after our arrival we had the first snow of the winter—a Wisconsin snowfall of about eighteen inches. We were totally unprepared for such an eventuality, and to complicate matters, Prince (our golden retriever) escaped at the height of the storm, and I took off after him. Visibility was so limited, the snowfall so heavy, and the wind so bitterly severe that I immediately lost sight of him, and within minutes I was completely disoriented. Eventually I found my way home, to be met by Jill and three tearful kids grieving the loss of their beloved Prince. "He's the only link with England," Jill sobbed. We had not had time to register him, and it seemed there was nothing we could do.

That night family prayers had a fervency and poignancy that was uncommon. Earnestly and tearfully the kids asked the Lord to please look after Prince while we uttered equally heartfelt "Amens." The storm cleared as suddenly as it had arrived. The sun shone brilliantly, and the landscape was buried in a deep layer of snow—it was a beautiful sight, like nothing we had ever seen in England. But how could we enjoy it when we knew that somewhere under the carpet of snow lay the frozen body of dear old Prince, whose reckless approach to life had finally led to his untimely death?

Two days passed slowly and sadly. The kids had no stomach for anything. Jill and I prayed that the Lord would intervene, if only to encourage the kids.

The phone rang. "Mr. Briscoe, do you own a golden retriever?"

"We did," I replied, being strictly honest.

"I think we have him in our dog pound," the man on the other end announced. Never having heard of a dog pound, I had no idea what he meant.

"You know, Mr. Briscoe, he has no registration tag on his collar."

"How do you know he's our dog?" I inquired, puzzled by the whole conversation.

"It's a funny thing. We saw the name 'Ray Hall' on his collar," he started to explain.

"Then he's not our dog," I interrupted.

"Well, we called the only Ray Hall in the Milwaukee directory, and he said he didn't own a dog but that he lived next door to you and you had just arrived from England with a retriever and he thought you had lost him. So he gave us your number, and I think you should come and take a look at him," he went on.

We bundled the kids into the car, hardly daring to hope. But on arrival at the pound there was Prince, large as life, wagging his tail as if trying to dislodge it. But I didn't understand the "Ray Hall" on his collar. So I took a look, and immediately I realized what had happened. Prince had worn his collar for years, and when it was new it had carried our English address—Capernwray Hall, Carnforth. The years had worn away everything but Ray Hall!

When I explained that to the kids I asked, "Do you think it was a coincidence?"

"No," they chorused.

"Do you think it was a coincidence that in a city of one and a quarter million people the only Ray Hall lived next door to us?"

"No," they shouted.

"Do you think it was a coincidence that Mr. Hall thought to mention our name?"

"No," they yelled.

"Then what do you think happened?" I asked.

"I think God heard and answered our prayers," answered David earnestly.

"Then let's thank him," said Jill. So we did.

Then Judy said, "We should thank Mr. Hall, too."

And Peter said, "What's a coincidence?"

That night Jill and I talked quietly about the events of the day, and together we agreed that in some strange way we had sensed the Lord's special care for the children in their new environment, and this we, independently of each other, had taken as yet another gracious seal on our decision. We were going to need it!

One day I mentioned to Jill that since we had arrived I had not seen some of the people who had been most enthusiastic about our call. "They must be out of town," she offered. I didn't think about it again until the first deacons' meeting. As I had never attended such a meeting I was quite eager to participate. The first item on the agenda was, "Resignation of Music Director and Organist."

To provide some background to the story, I must tell you that on the second or third Sunday night of my ministry I had gone into the sanctuary and waited for the choir and song leader to enter. Nobody came. So I stood up and said, "Has anybody seen the choir and their leader? They have apparently gotten lost." There was an awkward silence, and somebody whispered, "He quit."

"Oh really," I said, falling back on the standard noncommittal British response. "Well, where's the organist?"

"She's his wife, and she quit, too!" came the whispered response.

"Oh," I said with great good cheer, "I've always wanted to lead singing. Can anybody play the piano?"

Now the deacons were busy discussing the issue. I had no idea what was going on, so I listened for a while and then asked innocently, "What are we discussing?"

"Whether to accept the music director's resignation or not," I was told.

"What d'you mean accept it? He's resigned. What is there to accept?"

"This is his way of asking the new pastor for a vote of confidence," a deacon said.

"Well, tell him he hasn't got it," I replied, adding, "Why would I have any confidence in a fellow who quit without warning, notice, or explanation?" That did it. A heated debate broke out among the deacons, and I seemed to be the subject.

"Who does he think he is, anyway? Getting off the plane and trying to run the show?" someone asked.

"He was only responding to the 'vote of confidence' thing," someone else tried to explain, adding somewhat lamely, "Is that how you do it in England? If you resign you've resigned?"

"Exactly," I interjected.

"If you had any guts you'd address the issue fairly and squarely," I was then advised.

For the first time in a long time I saw red (my first deacons' meeting, remember!). "Are you accusing an ex-Royal Marine commando of being gutless?" I demanded, regretting it as soon as I had said it. The rest of the meeting passed by in a haze. I was horrified and mortified. Horrified at what I had heard, mortified by what I had said. On the way home in the chairman's car I noticed he was crying. I asked him, "What's the matter? What's going on?"

"Some of those men concluded when you had visa delays that we had made a mistake in calling you, and they wanted to cancel the call. They don't want you here!" he said softly.

I was stunned but heard myself responding, "Well, we came here because we believed God called us, and we'll stay till he calls us away." I said it, but I wondered how much I believed it. In all my life I had never felt so shocked.

The chairman, a dear friend to this day, prayed with me, hugged me (something I had to get used to in America), and said, "I'm sorry, Stuart. I thought I did right in not telling you." Then I remembered the missing faces and I understood their absence. They didn't think we should be there either.

Suddenly a bleakness like nothing we had known before entered our lives. We had left home and kindred, happily if not easily. We had uprooted family enthusiastically if not casually. We had "gone West" with a keen sense of moving to new horizons, only to discover them clouded and somber. We had responded to the call of God, as best we understood it, to discover the opposition of people as we had never before known it.

Where had we gone wrong? Which signals had we misread? Why was this happening? We had no answers, only questions. In retrospect I have little doubt that we overreacted. For one reason, we had never been in a pastoral situation before. We had no personal experience of the politics of ecclesiastical living and so were totally unprepared for our baptism into them. In addition, my ministry, because it had been itinerant, tended to be idealistic and theoretical—poor preparation for ministry in a local church, which by definition must be realistic and practical. Because we were sure of God's call, we assumed everybody would be equally sure of it; because we welcomed it and had acted upon it, we assumed everyone else welcomed it and was enthusiastically acting upon it.

In the midst of our disappointment and discomfort, however, we were wonderfully encouraged by those who really wanted us there. They showered us with kindness and encouraged us to dive in at the deep end of suburban American living. We soon discovered that the spartan, frugal lifestyle of Capernwray was very different from the much freer (free-spending and free-wheeling) lifestyle of the American suburbs. We were invited to parties, to country clubs to play tennis and golf, to the theater and the symphony—and we tried to respond. But as we had come from a scene where we rarely had interest in parties or money for theater or time for golf and tennis, our best efforts were sadly lacking. I couldn't get away from feeling guilty that life was so easy and fun-filled and lacking in the intensity to which I had been accustomed.

In a very short time, however, the work of the church became so demanding that while we learned from our new American friends how to "hang loose" a little, we were in no danger of going too far in that direction—there was too much to do. Slowly the warmth of the welcome of many people seemed to melt the chill of our sense of rejection and the enthusiastic response to our ministry began to overshadow all other considerations—for two or three months, anyway. Then we ran into another problem.

During one of my previous visits to Elmbrook to finalize arrangements, I had been invited on a Tuesday evening to something called "Forever Family." It was a group of young people who met in the home of church members Bob and Win Couchman. As I drove toward their home I noticed cars, mostly rusty, parked on both sides of the street. On arriving at the house I was surprised to find furniture stacked outside in the snow. As I tried to go inside I realized why the furniture was outside—the floor was wall-to-wall kids! They were children of the sixties—long hair, beards, guitars, blue jeans patched with the American flag, T-shirts, ornate crosses dangling from chains around their necks, and flowers behind their ears. Hardly your normal Sunday-morning congregation!

Presiding over this crowd were Bob and Win, a genial, gracious couple who, when some of their own kids became members of the counterculture, resisted the urge to resist, encouraging them instead to bring their friends home so Mom and Dad could meet them, talk to them, and show them their own brand of winsome Christianity. "Forever Family" was the result. I had a wonderful evening with the group and decided that if and when I ever was offered the pastorate here, one of my areas of concentration would be to encourage the integration of "Forever Family" into Elmbrook Church.

I had been working on a book called *Where Was the Church When the Youth Exploded?* much of which recounted the story of our work among similar young people in Europe, and my conviction that those who had become believers needed to be part of the church—and equally, the church needed those youngsters to be part of it! The church, in general terms, had the experience without the

177

enthusiasm; the youth, the enthusiasm without the experience. The former produced a dead orthodoxy; the latter, lively chaos. I believed the integration of the two would produce lively orthodoxy. That was the theory!

In practice I discovered that many of the "Forever Family" were less than enthusiastic about church, although very enthusiastic about Jesus. But eventually they agreed to attend a Sunday morning service. At that time the congregation numbered about five hundred and the "Forever Family" one hundred. They made quite a sight when they marched in, resplendent in their own special brand of finery, to sit with the suburbanites in their somewhat different brand of finery. Everybody was polite to everybody else, but things were a little tense. Unfortunately, as Jill has often explained to people, I am not particularly susceptible to atmosphere—I was so excited to have the kids there because I could work on one of my pet theories.

I was convinced that one of the hallmarks of the church is unity in diversity. There is nothing unusual about a society that has unity without diversity. Many organizations and most institutions operate on that principle. And there is nothing unusual about a diversity of people and interests making no attempt at unity. But my theory was, basically, if we can get totally different people (diversity) united in Christ (unity), people will see it and say, "Behold how these Christians love one another"—and they'll stand in line to join us.

Shortly after the "Forever Family" started to join in our church experience I was visited by one of the fine young businessmen in the church. He was all business as he came into my study one Saturday morning. Without any preamble he said, "Now about these young people you have brought into our church . . . "

"Strictly speaking, I didn't bring them in," I interjected.

". . . they are to be kept totally separate from our young people," he went on. "Do you understand?"

"I think so," I responded. "It's called the policy of separate development. In South Africa it's known as apartheid."

He looked surprised at the mention of apartheid but continued. "We have worked hard to get our kids away from that kind of young person, and we don't want you mixing them up again in church."

"I understand your concerns as I understand the rationale behind apartheid. Both are related to fear and prejudice, so while I understand what you're saying, I reject it. The Christian church cannot operate on those motivations, however real they may be."

To my surprise he listened, asked questions, and after I had outlined my understanding of the church's uniqueness in unity-diversity, he said, "Okay, I see what you mean. So what should we do about it?"

We spent the rest of the morning brainstorming and came up with an idea for a thirteen-week class called "Generation Bridge." It would be by invitation only, comprised of people from totally different segments of our fellowship. They would commit to attending all thirteen sessions, would study the Epistle of James, and they would not have a teacher, but each week two of their number (one older, one younger) would lead the study.

It worked like a dream. As soon as the class got under way we had a waiting list of people who wanted to be in the next class. The result was that representatives of different segments of the fellowship who would not naturally be attracted to each other or would naturally be repelled by each other took time to get to know each other. They also put themselves under the authority of Scripture and together began to apply some very straightforward teaching about life in the fellowship. The difference was remarkable.

At the end of the quarter we discovered that deep relationships had been formed. We held another class the next quarter and then, at their suggestion, discontinued it because, as they said, "We've dealt with all the issues, so now we don't need any more talking!"

◼◼◼◼◼◼

One day a young man named Tom, a student at Marquette University, asked if he could become a member of Elmbrook. He had completed the premembership class, and on the day he was to be received into membership he asked if he could address the congregation. I readily agreed, but a deacon who overheard the conversation said, "You're not going to let him speak, are you?"

"Yes," I replied. "If he has something to contribute to the fellowship, he should be encouraged to do so."

He certainly had something to contribute! That night, with his long hair neatly combed, wearing a clean T-shirt, jeans, and a cross that looked as if it had previously belonged to an archbishop, he spoke. "A few months ago I was pushing dope. Some people from this church befriended me. They said I was the most objectionable person they had ever met. But they stuck with me, and eventually I found the Savior they had introduced me to. They told me about Elmbrook, and I longed to come out here to meet all the people like them. One day I came. I must tell you in all honesty it was one of the biggest disappointments of my life."

He paused and the congregation became very, very still. Tom continued. "I was confronted on every hand by disinterest at best, and hostility at worst. You let me know I wasn't welcome, and I have to tell you I resented your attitude. I was hurt and I was angry." I looked around the congregation—everyone was listening. He had our attention, but I wondered where he was going.

"The reason I'm telling you all this is simply to confess the sin of my resentment against the congregation. This sin needs to be confessed publicly and corporately because it is against a body of believers and has been perpetuated in a public fashion."

A sense of relief seemed to come over the congregation. It was as if everybody had been holding their breath and now they collectively exhaled. But he had not finished.

"My anger against your resentment is my sin, and it has been confessed and forgiven. Your prejudice and rejection is your sin and needs to be confessed. If we're going to be the church, let's be the church. It is unlikely that I will ever look like many of you, and it is unlikely most of you will ever look like me, but that is not the point. I am committed to Christ, and I am committed to this church. The fact that I may not be committed to your lifestyle is not important. In fact, if you want to discuss it with me I believe I can make a better case for my lifestyle from the teaching of Jesus than I can for yours. But that is not the point."

With that he sat down. I preached that night to a sober, attentive congregation, and at the end I invited those present to take steps to deal with their resentments and their estrangements. They did in great numbers, and we began to see God do a great work of reconciliation and blessing.

That night when we finally arrived home, Jill and I looked at each other, hugged, and laughed.

"It's working!" she said.

"We're going to have a church," I replied. Shortly after this experience I wrote:

"All These Kids in Church"

How would you explain it?
The latest fad?
An emotional upheaval?
Communist infiltration?
Spiritual revival?
All those kids in church!
Unashamed,
Unabashed,
Undismayed,
Unbelievable!
Listening,
Learning,
Loving,
Yearning.
Togetherness,
Foreverness,
Warm smiles,
Quiet eyes,
Serene expression.
Sharing,
Caring,
Bearing,
Daring,
But where are the old folks?
Some with
Bowed head,
Faces red,
Fled!
Some dismayed,
Afraid,
Prayed and
Stayed.
Knees shaking,

182

Hearts breaking,
Efforts making,
Chances taking,
To believe,
To receive,
To achieve,
To relieve.
Willing,
Watching,
Waiting,
Worrying,
Saints.
White hair,
Long hair,
No hair,
Tinted hair
Bowed
In prayer.
Weeping together,
Reaping together,
Sowing together,
Growing together.
Lord's work,
Teamwork.
Worship,
Fellowship,
Relationship,
Stewardship,
Discipleship.
One body,
One Spirit,
One hope,
One Lord,
One faith,
One baptism,

One God,
One Father
Above them all,
Through them all,
And in them all,
Amen.

15

Being Firm, Fair, and Fun

Jill

S tuart, in typical fashion, tackled the teenage years, refusing to be intimidated. I, in typical fashion, was intimidated from the word *go*. Whereas Stuart's rules for parenting teens were "Be firm, be fair, and be fun," mine were "fear, freeze, and flap." I was just plain frightened all the time. On looking back it would be hard to tell you why. But fear doesn't need a reason to move into your life and take over. It was usually the fear of the invisible rather than the visible, the terror of the *what if* and the *what might be* if the *what if* happened. To live your days in the throes of the *what if* syndrome doesn't exactly lend itself to happy memories down the road!

I'm sure that part of my problem had to do with my own unrealistic expectations. I had to stop creating little pictures in my head of the kids waltzing through the traumas of their adolescent years with halos, wings, and ballet pumps. Ours were real children. I mean *real* ones. They were subject to their environment and peer pressure just as we were. They worked in their classrooms, for example, to a background of rock music (the teacher liked it on low, but nonstop), and, much to my chagrin, it didn't take very long for Dave's taste in music to fall in line. He didn't come home and switch on a tape of my favorite hymns, or even the latest Christian band for that matter.

Both Stuart and I had been writing for quite a while, and a publisher kept asking us to write a book together about teenagers.

"Why don't we do it?" Stuart asked.

I struggled to give him an answer. "Because—because—the kids aren't—aren't—"

"Aren't spiritual giants," my husband supplied, guessing my train of thought.

"Well—yes," I admitted.

"Giants are freaks," my husband commented. "I don't want freaky kids. Our kids are kids—let's do the book."

We never did, although all of the children have popped up regularly in book after book as a source of inspiration, education, and illustration. The older two wanted to be kept out of the limelight, while Pete enjoyed it thoroughly, bouncing into his dad's study one Sunday morning with a cheery, "Try and work me into the sermon today, Dad." When his dad did, Pete asked for royalties!

"If only God would lean out of heaven and tell me they are going to make it, I could relax," I complained. But God doesn't do that. He tells us to be the parents he has called us to be in his strength and promises to do his part. Driven to prayer (after discovering that manipulation didn't work), I began to realize I was only truly positive and confident when I'd been flat on my face before the Lord.

I began to make lists all over again. One had David's name at the top, one Judy's, and one Pete's. I wrote down in my imagination all I hoped and dreamed for my children, and as clearly as I'd heard his voice years ago in my little pink and white bedroom in England, I heard it all over again in my blue and white bedroom in America. "Give me the list, Jill." Now then, these lists were harder to let go of than the first one! But he helped me to release my grasp and stop clutching onto my hopes and dreams and let those same nail-pierced hands have them all.

I can say, though, that I never lost an overriding concern and intense desire to see them all love each other, as well as the Lord that Stuart and I loved. I knew I was safe praying those kinds of prayers for them because Jesus was praying prayers just like that as well.

Meanwhile, as I was working hard on my fears, freeze, and flap, Stuart was working hard being firm, fair, and fun. I could see he was having a wonderful time reveling in his growing friendship with his growing children, determined to believe the very best about them and for them.

The years took to their heels and began to speed away. I wanted to stop the clock and get off for a while. Here we were parenting together really for the first time. I loved the balance of a mom and a dad with their different perspectives and insights brought to bear on the huge challenge of seeing God create a spiritual sense inside this God-given legacy of love called children.

The first time David came running in from school and disappeared into his room to read his Bible without being told drew my tears. Leafing through that Bible some time later, he showed me the result of his quiet insistence to become a man Jesus loved. Page after page was colored and marked. "See, Mom," he confided, "Dad taught me—blue is for commands, green for promises, yellow for warnings, red for something about Jesus, and purple for something about me!"

Judy and I began to have confrontations of another sort. She wasn't into colored pencils and she wasn't into Navigators notes like I was. She wasn't into much of anything spiritual for a while and after a blowup told me, "Mom, you've got to let me find God my way." How could I do that and be a good Christian parent? I worried. How did I know her way would be as good as my way?

"How about my way?" the Lord asked me as I fervently prayed about our argument. I knew it had to be his way or it would never work at all. In the end, we parents cannot do the Holy Spirit's work for him even though we might try.

God's wisdom is such that he lets us begin to practice giving over control during the teen years, so we can really do a good job as college or work looms on the horizon and the birds get ready to fly the coop. Now I discovered I really had no option but to quit playing God. It was God's prerogative to be omnipresent—not mine! Omniscient and omnipotent, too. I couldn't go with Judy on her dates (she wouldn't let me, even though I asked), but he could—and would. He was omnipresent. I couldn't know who had written Dave a letter with hearts all over the envelope—seeing he snatched it eagerly and ran to his room to read it—but God knew. He was omniscient. And I had no power at all to enable my Pete to make right decisions at a school party after a game—where parents provided a barrel of booze—but God did. He was omnipotent.

Up to now it had been trust and obey, now it was trust and pray. Trust God, trust them, and trust Stuart and myself to do our job the best we possibly could and leave the rest to the Lord. We wouldn't do it all right, but we wouldn't do it all wrong either, I decided. Well, I decided that until I saw my kids fall in love! There's nothing quite as taxing as watching your children fall in love. First love is the very best and the very worst. They are helpless before its tidal influence. To see your children drowning in feelings that ebb and flow freely without their desire or permission is frightening, to say the least.

"They can't help how they feel," Stuart pointed out, practical as ever.

"First love is so sharp, Stu," I said. "I'd forgotten how it hurts." *It hurts when it's reciprocated and it hurts when it's rejected,* I mused. *It hurts with a pain deeper than any tummy ache.* When they were younger I had been able to make their tummy aches go away, but I couldn't touch their emotional pain now.

"If only the kids would fall for the right kids," I said earnestly to Stuart. He looked at me as if I was strange.

"Who are the right kids?" he inquired.

"Well, not the ones they are busy falling for," I ventured.

Stuart laughed. "You mean you don't think they are the right ones, and you know the ones they should be falling for?"

"Well," I began, somewhat defensively, "yes."

"You're not on their level," Stuart responded seriously. "Trust them to know the guidelines we've tried to teach them to look for. Relax and enjoy it."

There he was again, busy being fair, firm, and fun, while I was in a perfect flap, frozen in my fear! Somehow, with his help, I was able to work through some of my trauma in time to really test it all, as our three headed happily, bright-eyed and bushy-tailed, into their college years.

As the day approached when David would set sail for the campus, all sorts of people began to murmur the words *empty nest syndrome* sympathetically in my ear. That I didn't need to hear. Why, we had two left at home and a good five years at least until I had to fight that particular battle.

One day I hit a bird on the road. I don't know why, but it really upset me. I hate to see any of God's wonderful creatures in trouble. The children were with me, and we all got out of the car and picked the little thing up. Its little heart was beating furiously, and you could see the soft feathers on its breast lifting as the tiny organ pumped away. Pete was the most upset. "I think it's got a broken wing, Mom," he said, tears in his big brown eyes. "Let's take it to the animal hospital." We tended the little thing, and the children nursed it lovingly back to health. The day it flew away, I remember getting a flash of inspiration.

For a little while our home had been a safe nest for the broken creature, and, with a lot of tender loving care and sincere prayers on its behalf, it was now whole again and doing all the things it had been designed by its Creator to do. The parable came home to me. As I faced the college years I knew I didn't need to fear the empty nest syndrome anymore. In fact, I knew enough about people to realize no Christian couple should ever be found guilty of having an empty nest. Surely our world was far too full of birds with broken wings!

I thought about Stuart and me and the different seasons of our love. The springtime was past, and we were approaching the end of the warm summer days of child rearing. Now autumn love, weighted with its rich colors of the changing season, waited for us. It would be different, but it would be rich in a variety of ways as surely as autumn was different from spring. This lesson, however, didn't save me from any of the natural pain as the process began to take place. No tree likes to lose its leaves.

One big thing that helped tremendously was the talking that Stuart and I were able to do together as the time approached to get the kids launched.

"Let's decide that the day they leave the house is the day they become adults. This way they know we know we've entered a new phase of our relationship," suggested my husband.

"What difference will it make?" I wanted to know.

"Well, for a start we won't ask them where they are going when they go out, and we won't question the time they come back," he said. "We won't need to ask them who's on the phone anymore either," he added. "It won't mean they can treat our home like a hotel, with no regard for our schedule or rules, but they will know if we treat them like adults, we expect them to behave like adults."

I sat there very still. They were so very young when they went away. Only eighteen years of age—mere babes. How could we consider them suddenly to be adults? The impression of their youthfulness wasn't helped very much when we began to take them up to school either.

"Stuart, what are all these little kids doing at college?" I asked in shock, gazing around at the typical incoming freshmen milling around. He laughed.

"You're getting old when you notice how young the policemen or college kids are, Jill," he quipped. "I was in the Marine commandos at their age."

I suppose those initial deliveries to the college campus will always be etched on my mind. "Feel free to go as slow as you like, Dad," Judy teased through her tears as we set off for the three-hour trip to Wheaton College. I tried to comfort myself that I would have been a lot more upset if she hadn't shed a tear and was dying to leave home!

All our children had been given the option to choose a secular or Christian college, and all had opted to go to a Christian school. At that time all three didn't know for sure which direction to go, and so, unsure if they would ever go on to do any biblical training, they decided to get it along with their undergraduate work. All three had had good experiences in a secular high school seeing their friends accept Christ and finding out what it meant to stand up for their faith in that kind of environment. Now, however, they wanted to integrate their faith into whatever training God would give them for their life's work. We were more than happy with their choices and promised to help them as much as we could.

The boys weathered their college years in typical fashion. Dave went for a business major and Bible minor, saying that he wasn't sure whether the Lord wanted him to be a businessman with a ministry or a minister who was businesslike! Pete "knew" from the start he'd end up in full-time Christian work and so took a communications major and Bible minor. It was Judy, however, who struggled most.

Judy had always been our good child. "We need never worry about Judy," I remember saying happily and confidently to Stuart when she was quite young. "She only wants to please us." We didn't know that a great desire to please could be a problem of its own particular sort. In Judy's mind nothing she achieved—or ever overachieved—was good enough. She didn't feel it was good enough for her daddy or her mommy, and it certainly wasn't good enough for Judy. What do you do when an *A* or even an *A+* is never enough?

Unaware of our little Type A daughter struggling with a sense of inadequacy, we bolstered up the boys who "should have" been feeling at least a little inadequate in some areas of their schooling and gave all too few affirmations to Judy.

On one occasion, as report cards were being discussed, her brother said, "The trouble with you, Judy, is that you don't even know what shape a *B* is."

"Neither do you, but for different reasons," Stuart quietly responded with a laugh and something less than total accuracy.

When Judy went to Wheaton she was already well on the way to developing an anorexic mindset—it was in the days before anorexia had become a household word, and we had absolutely no idea what was happening.

After a traumatic visit to school, Stuart and I stood in our kitchen sipping hot coffee and simply looking at each other. We didn't have a clue what was going on. We only knew Judy was in deep, deep trouble physically, though her academic record was almost perfect.

"She looked terrible, Stu," I said desperately. "What can be the matter?"

Then we received a phone call from the big, handsome boy who had fallen in love with our little girl during the second week of school. His name was Greg, and they had dated for a year or so when he asked if he could bring Judy home that weekend and talk to us.

Sitting at our dining room table, we were introduced to our future son-in-law, though we didn't know it then. Near tears, he told us that what he was about to do would probably finish off his relationship with Judy, but if something wasn't done, we would all lose her.

It was extremely hard to hear. Greg had in typical fashion done his research. He produced a book and told us he was convinced she was manifesting symptoms of *anorexia nervosa*. He told us about Judy's compulsive behavior—her almost fanatical running regime, her weight loss, and her eating habits. "I don't know how she's doing what she's doing on an occasional lettuce leaf," he said desperately. We didn't know either.

As Stuart had to catch a plane, he asked Judy to take him to the airport and on the way asked her to promise she would not allow her weight to go below what it was until we'd had time to think and talk about it all together.

I had feared our children might get into trouble for being bad—it had never occurred to me that any of them could get into trouble being good! Judy's huge desire to please and her perceptions of our expectations had serious consequences.

How we thank God for Greg, for Wheaton, and for some sensitive, godly professors who stepped in and counseled our little girl back to health again. And how we thank God for each other and the resources we had of skilled friends and helpers to see our part in redressing the situation. It seems incredible now some thirteen years later, with Judy finishing off her Ph.D. in psychology, to look back and realize the confusion and pain we worked through together. How delicate a balance needs to be maintained in parenting before the children are grown—and afterward in growing as friends and confidants.

Now that all the children were off to school, I began to accept more of the opportunities I had taken in small measure while the children had been in their teens. Stuart was the one who encouraged me. Now *I* began to travel and Stuart stayed behind to keep the home fires burning. I began to find out a tiny part of the other side of the picture: It was lonely out there. And scary. I had more problems with inadequacy than I thought possible. And the biggest fear of all was the way I had to get where I was going! Hardly ever having flown at all before coming to the States, I now faced that challenge nearly every week.

If you, like me, are afraid of flying, I won't need to describe my antics—sitting in the aisle seat if the plane looked as though it needed balancing up a bit, refusing to sit by the wings because they flapped so much, going into a tailspin when the noises changed in the cabin. I felt literally sick every time I got on board and had to clutch onto Stuart's arm. On a particular flight over Vancouver one day, he said, "Jill, you won't go to heaven one day before you're meant to. And it's no good clutching onto me—I'm going up and down as well!"

His logic didn't help me that time. I knew I wouldn't go to heaven one moment before I was meant to, but my problem was each time I flew I was convinced that was when I was meant to! And even though I felt rather guilty with the thought, I didn't want to go to heaven just yet.

I wanted to see the kids through college and into the arms of their chosen spouses, if that was to be God's gift to them. I wanted to learn to be firm, fair, and fun before I hit eighty years of age. I actually wanted to hit eighty years of age. I wanted to partner Stuart through the phenomenal church growth we were seeing at Elmbrook and learn to be a halfway effective ministry wife. I wanted to write and dream and dare and do together, and I didn't want it all to end—just yet. It didn't—as you can see—but it took a real leap of faith for me to let God deal with my fear. He did it as he's always done it—through the Word and by his Spirit. Is there any other way? I don't know any!

16

Is There a Family in the House?

Stuart

Having spent a sizable part of my life working with teenagers, I was reasonably confident as I embarked on the task of raising my own—despite the horror stories that seemed to abound on every hand. Naturally, there were going to be major differences between dealing with my own flesh and blood and someone else's progeny. It was one thing to have teenagers for a limited amount of time before sending them home, but an entirely different thing to have nowhere to send them because we were home! And, of course, as a leader of young people I had been able to preserve, through the nurturing of my natural British reserve, a certain distance, which I fondly imagined had bred an ill-defined mystique, deserving of the utmost respect.

But now there was no distance (we shared bathrooms), little reserve (they borrowed and failed to return my clothes), less mystique ("leave Dad alone, he'll get over it in a few minutes!")—and accordingly, respect was rarely given. But it could be earned.

I suppose parents, who usually learn their craft by doing, often look back to their own upbringing for ideas and models. While it is a given that most adults can remember

197

the faults in their parents' approach and vow to avoid them at all costs, they nevertheless tend to maintain much of what they assimilated and consciously or unconsciously transfer it to their own children. This was certainly true in Jill's and my experience.

For instance, my parents were strict and hard-working with little time and less inclination for fun. As their resources of time and money were limited and their commitments to service were many, entertainment ("worldliness") was rarely factored into our lives and was actually looked upon with suspicion. So, for example, while I was a better-than-average athlete and played most sports for my school, not only did my parents never once see me play; they actually worked hard to ensure that I remembered there were far better ways of spending my time and energy.

I was less than happy about being told repeatedly, "Bodily exercise profiteth little," and when I pointed out, somewhat tentatively, that it at least profited a little, I was rebuked for my impertinence. So I decided that when my own teenagers came along I would build into their lives as much fun as possible and I would share it with them, if they would permit me.

Fortunately, Jill's parents had greatly encouraged her in these areas, so she was most enthusiastic about the kids' lives being full of opportunities to enjoy their growing years to the maximum. However, she had been given great freedom during her teen years, and she was very much aware of the way she had abused it and was afraid that our kids might do the same. She wanted to see a firm hand on our kids. I knew a lot about this sort of thing, and while I hadn't always appreciated it when I was subjected to it, I had no doubt in my own mind that I had needed it and had benefitted from it. So "be fun and be firm" became part of our teenager-rearing philosophy.

While I had reacted against the strictness of my parents and wanted more fun, and Jill had reacted against the openness of her parents and wanted more firmness, we were both appreciative of both sets of parents' commitment to being as evenhanded in their dealings as possible. We liked their attempts to be fair and added this to our basic approach: "Be firm, be fair, be fun." Not for one moment would I give the impression that we always succeeded in this endeavor, but we did at least have some idea of where we were trying to go.

KKKKKK

In my particular situation as a highly visible pastor of a church, it followed naturally that the kids were marked out as preacher's kids both in the church and in the community. We had seen and heard enough examples of preachers' kids being subjected to unrealistic expectations—leading to resentment and eventual rejection of the church and the faith—that we knew we had to be perfectly fair in our expectations of them.

Many times we consciously avoided what others had failed to avoid (for readily understandable reasons) and that was the temptation to say to our kids, "Now what do you think the people will think if they hear that you have (fill in the blank), or if they see you with (fill in the blank)?" When parents are trying desperately to corral their teens, they tend to use whatever lasso is available, only to discover that sometimes they have roped themselves. So we told the kids that they were not answerable to the church, neither were they accountable to the community; they were accountable to us as their parents, and we would commit ourselves to giving them as normal an experience as possible in the abnormal fish tank of the preacher's family. It went without saying, of course, that they were responsible, as young believers, to the Lord, and as citizens to their community, and as church members, to the church.

But it was not always easy. On one occasion Jill and I were away for a couple of days, and we asked a fine young couple to move into our home and oversee the kids. On our return the young couple asked to speak with us. They sat us down and poured out their dismay at the way our children had behaved, particularly as they were "pastor's children." We were horrified, of course, and called in the children immediately after the couple left. (They were actually waiting outside the door, suspecting what was happening, and eager to say their piece!)

Judy, ever vocal, said, "I suppose they've been telling you what bad kids we are."

"I'm afraid so, Judy," I replied.

"Well, Dad, let me tell you something. Not only do they not understand teenagers, they don't even like them."

"Be that as it may, Judy, they said they would never look after you again," I said severely.

"Good," all three chorused. "We wouldn't have let them anyway!"

Sensing something vaguely resembling a mutiny I said, "That's enough of that kind of talk."

"Dad, you know we're not bad kids," said David, the young man of few words. "We were just being normal."

"Maybe normal in your eyes isn't good enough," I suggested.

"It would have been normal in your eyes too, Dad," said David.

"You see, while they were here they treated us like little kids, and we started to behave like little kids. But you treat us like adults, and we try to behave like adults!" Judy added quickly.

The conversation went on for some time; we dealt with the excesses of their behavior, spelled out the requirements for future experiences, and agreed to David's further suggestion, "Dad, I think we are old enough not to need a baby sitter if you two are only gone for two nights. We would be fine on our own. Why not trust us, and we'll rise to the occasion." So, taking a deep breath, we did!

On our return after the first experiment with this arrangement, the kids were arguing about some triviality or other, so I said, "If this is how you behave while we are away, it is obvious you are not ready to be on your own." Judy replied immediately, her brothers nodding furious assent, "Dad, while you were away we were so good. We knew we had to pull together and we did. Dave was so sweet, and Pete actually helped for once. But now that you're back, we're just relaxing a bit." They were learning responsibility, developing caring attitudes, and when strictly necessary, cooperating rather than competing.

◄◄◄◄◄◄

On one occasion, as I was basking in the fact that I, the father of three teenagers, had learned how to be scrupulously fair to them, Dave shattered my illusion.

"The trouble with you, Dad, is you're prejudiced," he volunteered.

Knowing full well that I certainly was not prejudiced (except against prejudiced people!), I spluttered indignantly, "What do you mean I'm prejudiced? I . . ."

"You're prejudiced against the kind of music I like, and you've never bothered to listen to it. And you make all kinds of comments about the way the people in these groups live, but you don't like it when I say that Mozart was no saint either!" he interrupted.

He's right, said a little voice within.

"You're right, Dave," I admitted, looking around the table at Jill, who didn't seem to know whether to laugh or cry, and the three kids who were waiting with bated breath to see how the "old man" would react to this unexpected piece of unsolicited home truth.

"Well, that's not fair, Dad, and you're always telling us you want to be fair," Dave added.

"What do you want me to do?" I inquired.

"Just try listening to our kind of music for once."

"Your kind, not our kind," Judy added, setting some distance between her tastes and those of her older brother.

"Exactly," I said, sensing that I might have a chance to divide and conquer.

"But you don't listen to my kind either," said Judy, squashing my momentary advantage.

"Mine neither," added Pete for good measure.

"Mine neither," added Jill, quite unnecessarily in my opinion.

"All right," I said, recognizing defeat. "This is what we'll do. In the future during the evening meal we'll take turns choosing background music. The only condition is that the volume is controlled so that we can talk without bursting a larynx and listen without bursting an eardrum."

"That's fair," the family agreed, and so that is what we did.

We also agreed (except Dave) that his favorite rock groups were incomprehensible, that Judy's choices were too sentimental (she disagreed), that Jill's were too old-fashioned (Jill didn't agree), that Pete didn't know what he liked (Pete agreed), and that Beethoven gave everyone a headache (except me!). The nice thing about this was that a potential barrier had been turned into a bridge leading away from alienation to new levels of trust and understanding.

Family mealtimes became the scene of another family distinctive—the gripe session. As our kids were more or less normal, sibling rivalry was a readily recognizable part of family life. It usually operated rather volcanolike, building up pressure under the surface until finally erupting. After one or two eruptions that were not very pretty and certainly not at all constructive, it was determined (by me) that we would call a family meeting periodically for the express purpose of dealing with family members' objections.

The meeting was carefully structured. Every member of the family was given the opportunity to express any complaints or objections to any other family member. A certain time limit for the complaint was allotted. At the end of the complaint, the one against whom the complaint was leveled could ask for clarification and after that make a defense. Then the family would be free to give their input, and suggestions would be made. If there seemed to be no general agreement, a vote could be taken, but Father had veto powers, which, for the good of his own health and well-being, he never exercised!

Actually, more often than not the session would dissolve in laughter and rare good humor. But underlying the procedure was a firm conviction, managed by a firm hand, that family dissension was not acceptable and should be handled in such a way that relationships would be safeguarded and enriched, rather than damaged.

Jill and I also administered a firm hand in the area of church attendance. We made it clear that because ours was a Christian family, commitment to a church and its life was to be normative. We explained that this was true whether or not we lived in a preacher's home. In other words, church attendance was expected and required, not because Dad was the preacher, but because the family was Christian.

However, as parents we realized we not only should spell out the nonnegotiables but also give our teenagers some flexibility in order to make their own decisions. So we told them Sunday morning attendance was mandatory, even if they had been out late on Saturday night. (Our kids started a tradition that still stands in our church: After their senior prom—which for some inexplicable reason required them to stay up all night—they attended church in tuxedos and formals.) Sunday evening was optional, provided they could show good reason why they should not be there. They were also to plan on one mid-week activity of a Christian orientation, but they were completely free to choose which one. During our kids' teen years we had very few arguments over these rules, and the kids seemed to think there was a mixture of "firm and fair" in the arrangements. I certainly did, but then I had figured it all out in the first place!

The fun part of family life came in many different ways. Peter, our humorist, was always ready for a laugh even at the most inappropriate moments. On one occasion something had gone wrong in the family which required Father's firm and fair hand. Unfortunately, Father had had a bad day at the office (which he had forgotten to leave there) so there was clear evidence that it might spill over into a bad evening in the family. Father delivered his soul in no uncertain terms, issuing veiled threats of life imprisonment and other appropriate punitive actions, punctuated by resounding thumps on the table for emphasis, and the rest of the family was bludgeoned into a wary silence.

Except for Peter. While Jill, eyes filled with tears, looked anxiously to see what further unreasonable length I might go to, and Dave and Judy fixed their eyes firmly on their soup, Pete happily suggested, "Okay, now that that's over, let's all think of our favorite joke and tell it." There was a horrified silence, broken moments later when I burst out laughing, grasping the opportunity my son had unwittingly given to me to escape from the ridiculous corner I had backed myself into. He's done it more than once since that day, and the family is grateful.

Balancing being firm and being fun is not easy. On one occasion Pete brought home a report card that called for a degree of fatherly firmness. It was duly administered in no uncertain terms. I explained to him that not only were his grades unsatisfactory in that they reflected he was working well below his capacity, but the comments in the margin showed that his teachers were also dissatisfied with his behavior. Certain sanctions were imposed on him to reinforce the point, and he left the room duly chastened.

However, as he went I had a twinge of conscience, so I called him back and said, "Pete, I have to tell you in all honesty that at your age I brought very similar report cards home, and I'm not proud of it now. That's why I have spoken so firmly to you about it." He looked slightly surprised that I had admitted that my behavior had been as unsatisfactory as his, gave me a grateful look (presumably because I had tried to be honest), and left.

The incident was soon forgotten until the end of the next semester when he came into my study, put an envelope on my desk, and said with a mischievous grin, "Here you go, old man, another report card just like yours." Now that kind of impertinence cannot be disregarded, but it takes some handling when you are struggling not to laugh at his nerve!

Perhaps the most enjoyable times with our teenagers were spent when we made special time available to each one individually. Once we hit on the idea, however, we quickly discovered that to be effective, the event chosen had to be acceptable to them, at a time that fit into their schedules. Judy told me after I had blocked off time in my calendar to spend an evening with her, "Dad, I appreciate your doing this, but it would have been nice if you had checked with me first. I can't come with you because I have a date that night."

To my astonishment I discovered not only that she had an engagement book and a social calendar, but also that some young man had appeared on the scene who apparently rated ahead of me. I said something inappropriate, which exposed my hurt feelings. To which Judy responded, "Dad, it's not that time with you is less important than my date; it's just that I have a prior commitment and you've taught us to keep the commitments we make." Oh the joys of having teenagers who commit themselves to raising their parents properly! Anyway, we settled on another date, and went to a movie, then to dinner, sitting late into the night, talking heart to heart.

Time with Dave and Pete was usually reserved for sporting events—sometimes watching, sometimes playing. We'd go for a run, play racquetball, play a round of golf, watch a baseball game, and always finish up eating and talking. On one occasion I said to Pete, "What have we talked about so far this evening?"

"Basketball, football, baseball, hockey, and golf," he replied promptly.

"Right," I replied, adding, "have you noticed that we have not talked about anything significant?"

"Now that you mention it."

"Why d'you think that should be?" I queried.

Without hesitation he replied, "Because I can't think of anything significant I'm interested in!"

We both laughed because we knew it was not true. Whenever the kids had significant concerns they brought them up, and rarely did they object if Jill and I felt important matters needed to be brought to their attention.

█████

When each of the kids graduated from high school I made arrangements to take them with me on one of my overseas tours of ministry. Dave and I traveled to Britain, Sri Lanka, Singapore, Hong Kong, Japan, and Hawaii. Judy and I made a similar trip, missing Sri Lanka and Japan but adding Bangladesh and China. Pete decided that he wanted to go to Australia and told me he would wait until my next trip there. We were able to add Singapore, Hong Kong, and China to his experience.

One of the lasting benefits of these times together was that all three of them told me in different ways that, while they had believed it was all right for me to be away from home so much doing the Lord's work, it was only when they saw the kind of thing I was doing firsthand that they began to appreciate what had been happening.

I will always remember Dave coming to me after I had preached one night in the crowded National Theatre in Singapore and saying with shining eyes. "Dad, this is great. I'm so glad you have spent your life doing this, and I'm so glad that I could come and see it." Looking at my eldest son, soon to leave for college, I wondered what he would spend his life doing. I also wondered what role I would fulfill in guiding and directing him. I pondered the fact that a major part of my life was spent helping people discern God's will and encouraging them to follow through and do what he wanted them to do.

But I felt an inner sense of panic as I looked at Dave that night. I knew that he looked to me with high regard—he never said so in words; he always said so in deed. I was also aware that my personality could be overpowering, particularly for a young son who wanted to please his dad. I feared imposing my will on him; I dreaded the thought that I might subtly or not so subtly let him know what my expectations were for him. The one comforting thought in all this was that I genuinely did not know of any expectations I had for him, and therefore, I concluded it was unlikely that I would betray them to him.

As a result of my own uncertainty in this area, I decided that I would not say anything about careers to him. But I did tell him that he could choose to go either to a state university or Christian college, though I would give him a short list to choose from, since I would be paying! The college decision looked fine, but the silence I imposed on the career area had its limitations. It was some time later that I dared to broach the subject of career, and then I did it most apologetically.

"Dave," I said, during one of our get-togethers, "I hope you don't think that I have been imposing my will on you regarding what you do with your life."

He looked totally nonplussed and said, "What are you talking about?"

"Well," I responded somewhat lamely, "I always had a fear that I might get in the way of God's guidance in your life."

"How would you do that?" He seemed puzzled.

"By telling you what I thought you should do. In fact, I've been so scared of doing that that I've tried to say nothing."

To my amazement he responded, "That explains it."

"Explains what?"

"I've been wondering what was wrong with you because you spend your time giving other people advice and you never said a word to me. I've been waiting for you to start!" We had a great session after we finally got things on track, and I found that all he needed from me was a nod of affirmation that the things he had been thinking made sense.

"I don't honestly know whether I want to be a businessman or a minister. You've been both, and I think that's neat. But I do know that if I'm a businessman I want to have a ministry, and if I'm a minister I want to be businesslike. So I want to get a degree in business and then perhaps go to Bible school if I go into business. On the other hand, if I go into the ministry I'll go to graduate school for an M.Div. anyway," he explained.

Thank you, Lord, I breathed silently, looking at the earnest young teenager whose life was coming together beautifully according to the good hand of the Lord our God upon him.

Because Dave and I had paved the way, it was easier to be involved in the important decisions concerning Judy and Pete. Some of my most treasured memories are of heart-to-heart talks with our own young people, who were eager to discover and do God's will.

❌❌❌❌❌❌

A few years later I found myself directly involved in helping Dave make some more big decisions. He had met and fallen in love with a beautiful young woman, a dedicated believer, the daughter of a pastor. Debbie had become very dear to us in the all-too-infrequent visits she had made to our home. We were planning to take a group of people to the Mediterranean to study the journeys of Paul, and we invited Dave and Debbie to come with us. They made it clear to me that they wanted to talk, and not being totally out of touch with reality despite my advancing years, I arranged to meet with them as soon as we set sail from Piraeus.

With the Greek coastline as a backdrop we sat on deck and talked about engagement and marriage. They looked so young and strangely vulnerable, but I had no hesitation in encouraging them to go ahead if they were sure in their hearts that they wanted to spend the rest of their lives together. I reminded Dave that a common courtesy required him to ask Debbie's parents if they would approve of them getting engaged. They called from Galilee, bought a ring in Haifa, and got engaged in the Garden of Gethsemane. All very exciting and romantic and clearly of the Lord, as the succeeding years have proved.

I'm not much for cliches, but I rather like the one that says, "We haven't lost a son, we've gained a daughter." In the case of Dave and Debbie, and the subsequent marriages of our other children, we have embraced our children's spouses as enthusiastically as they have apparently embraced us.

I'm not sure why, but officiating at the marriage of my daughter was a much more emotional experience than fulfilling the same function for both of my sons. It certainly was not because I love my sons less than my daughter or my son-in-law less than my daughters-in-law. It probably has something to do with the special bond that develops between a girl and the first man in her life.

Judy's and my relationship got off on the wrong foot when I decided she was a boy before her birth and was flabbergasted when proven wrong. But whatever deficiencies there may have been in my prognosticating powers, they had been thoroughly compensated for from the moment I first held her and all through the intervening years. Particularly on our trip around the world: She was dreadfully ill in Bangladesh, homesick in India, lonely in Hong Kong, tired out most of the time, and anorexic all the time. Yet we were thrown together and had to care for each other.

210

I will never forget seeing her ill and frightened lying on the back of a truck, the only transport available to get her from Manikgang to Dacca in Bangladesh, and realizing that she was all my responsibility. Very little medical help was available, and I had put her in this situation. We clung to each other literally and metaphorically as never before, prayed as never before, and learned to love each other as never before.

But while my relationship with my daughter was special, I was blessed in my relationship with my two sons in that I had the opportunity to work with them as youth pastors on the church staff. One day while I was contemplating the need to find a new pastor to oversee the junior high school ministry, I was suddenly struck with the thought that Dave would be ideal. *But I couldn't recommend him to the elders,* I thought, *it would look like nepotism! Nepotism?* the other half of my brain responded. *Nepotism is granting favors to nephews. He's your son, not your nephew, and anyway, I can't see the favor in being made responsible for a couple of hundred junior high kids!*

Nevertheless, I dismissed the thought until later that evening when an elder called and said, "I suddenly thought this morning that we don't need to look any further than Dave for our new youth pastor." So I didn't. With a certain degree of self-consciousness I brought the matter up to the elders, who considered the perception of nepotism aspect and decided it was not an issue. Then one of them said, "We've all known Dave since he was a kid. I can't think of anybody I would rather have influencing my youngsters, and I also think we need a model of a father and son working together." So the council agreed to extend a call to my son Dave. It was an exciting and unnerving moment—the whole church would now not only watch us in a family situation but also in a senior pastor/youth pastor relationship. Dave and I discussed it all very carefully, prayed together, and came to a solid conclusion that we should go ahead.

Dave, greatly supported and assured by Debbie, served with us for three years, during which time he showed clear pastoral skills and good administrative ability and made a great contribution to a fine youth ministry. He acquitted himself so well that when he left to pursue theological studies I didn't hesitate to talk to the elders about Pete taking his place. The elders didn't hesitate either. In fact, the only grumble I heard from them was that we'd only produced two sons.

Pete built on Dave's work and brought his own brand of leadership to the group of young people. He stayed with me for four years before leaving to pursue his theological studies. On his final Sunday at Elmbrook, I publicly thanked him and Libby for their work and asked him to pass on a few words to his successor. He strode to the pulpit and said, "You all know my father preaches sermons with three points, all alliterative, and my mother writes poetry. I am a mixture of both, so here is a poem in three points!" He then delivered a very funny and very moving statement of what it means to serve the Lord. The entire congregation laughed, and some cried as together we responded to the evidence of God's work in our children.

Laughter and tears have characterized the years spent with our children. Much laughter, few tears, some sorrows, many joys, occasional rough spots, numerous delightful times—my memories of my kids are rich and precious. I'm grateful to God for his gracious work in them, and I'm grateful to them for making the task of being a "Firm, Fair, and Fun Father" a deep and satisfying joy.

17

"Those That God Has Joined Together"

Jill

*J*udy's finals at Wheaton were over. Exhausted, she came out of the lecture hall and ran right into Greg, who told her her dad was on the phone. "Judy," Stuart said softly, "I hate to do this to you directly after your finals, but I have to tell you some really hard news. Nanna has died."

Judy had always been exceptionally close to my mother. Maybe it was because she was the only granddaughter among five grandsons, or maybe it was because she alone of our three children had begged for all the extra time she could get with her Nanna over extended holiday periods, and they had bonded in an unusual way. I don't know—all I know is she loved my mother as much as I did, and I've always been thankful to her for that. What a miracle.

It had been hard for Judy to say good-bye to her Nanna when we left England. It had been doubly wrenching for me, knowing about my mother's claustrophobic fear of flying and therefore the reality of the situation—Peggy would never visit us in the States. And she never did. However, God provided the funds to visit her, and I took the boys and Judy with me through the years. In addition, Judy and her close friend Kerry had spent three wonderful extra weeks enjoying Nanna when they were fifteen, and again a close encounter of the very best kind had taken place.

Judy was devastated when Stuart gave her the bad news, for none of us had been aware of Mother's imminent death. It had been awfully hard trying to get facts three thousand miles away. Indeed, the reports from the doctor were positive, indicating she would be in poor but passable health for a good while.

Alerted in my spirit to the truth of Mother's condition, I had begun to want to visit her. Stuart and I were slated to go to Africa on a tour of ministry, visiting several work sites of the Sudan Interior Mission. Stuart's passport was being renewed for the trip, but we decided I should go to England and see Mother while she was still well and meet him in Africa later. While I was with her, she died. I was there when the angels came for her, and I "almost" heard the voice of him who is the Resurrection and the life calling her home. I only know the little bedroom was alive with divine activity, and I wasn't surprised when I saw Peggy stop breathing.

As I watched her go, a huge sense of spiritual comprehension swept over me. Jesus died that death might die. Jesus actually had to die for this to be accomplished—I knew that as fact, but I never realized it quite as I did at that moment. Watching Mother struggle for her last earthly breath, I clung onto her hand, crying and saying, "You mean, Lord, you did this for me!" It was terrible, yet it was wonderful, too. As Jesus stood outside the grave of Lazarus long ago and called his name, saying, "Lazarus, come out," I knew Jesus was standing here now calling for Peggy to "come out." And, like Lazarus, "she that was dead came out the other side of death, bound hand and foot with graveclothes."

Reading that passage a half hour after my mother's death, my heart leapt with joy at the words, "And Jesus said to those who stood by—loose him (her, in this case) and let her go." With the eye of faith I could see the angels unwinding Peggy's graveclothes and letting her go—into Daddy's arms and heaven. But now the Mother Space had to be dealt with. I didn't like the idea of being the mother now that mine had gone. Even though I was in my forties and my mom was old and ill, she was still my mother. She always was "there," giving me a sense of security, loving and praying for me always. I felt safe while she was alive—unsafe now that she had gone, and here I was alone with it! Stuart couldn't come to me—his visa wasn't ready. A funeral had to be arranged (my sister and I had decided I would make the arrangements) and I tried my best to do it, struggling with the searing loss of the mother I adored.

I had never quite been able to share my discoveries of Jesus with Peggy and was almost paralyzed now with guilt because of that, even though I had come to terms with the fact that only when she went to be with the Lord would she really understand. Waking up the morning after her death, I remember feeling as though an enormous weight had lifted from my shoulders and saying softly, "Oh Peggy— now—now you understand me, don't you? Now you know what happened to me twenty years ago. Wait a bit and I'll be there, and then we'll talk about it at last."

Thousands of miles away, in a phone box at Wheaton College, Judy said to her daddy, "Let me go to Mom, Dad."

"That's exactly what I wanted to ask you to do," Stuart replied. What none of us knew at that time was that Greg had bought a ring and had planned to "pop the question" that very weekend.

And so, standing at Manchester Airport the very next day, I watched my tall, long-legged, sweet, beautiful Judy coming toward me, tears streaming down her face. "Mom, I'm so sorry," she cried, clinging to me, "so very, very sorry." We stood there forever it seemed, finding the deep emotional pain a strange place to experience our relationship of womanhood together. We stood locked up in our mutual, personal grief, as we mourned a mother and grandmother we would always love and forever miss.

The funeral came and went, drawing my dear sister Shirley and me together as never before, and I put Judy back on a flight to happier things—a belated engagement to the love of her life and a final semester of school. I joined Stuart in Liberia, and we had a healing five weeks of ministry together.

It took me half that time to be able to talk about Peggy's death with Stuart. The feelings and pain were too deep. I couldn't bear to dig down to find the words. My nerves were too raw. Too many times each day the pictures of the death scene rudely intruded unbidden into my mind. I didn't know how to cope with the "groanings" inside me that couldn't be uttered.

Reading the account of Lazarus all over again, I saw a verse I'd missed: "Jesus groaning in himself came to the grave." There it was. Now I knew what that meant. These deep, deep groans that didn't have a voice, that began somewhere down in the bottom of my soul and eventually worked their way out—crushing my heart, contracting my stomach, and sending waves of breathless pain over my head. These groans were the same groans that Jesus experienced when he stood at the grave of someone he loved. He understood.

Stuart understood, too. He, like me, had "groaned" twice already. Lying in his arms one night, in the incredible heat of the sub-Sahara, I was able to talk at last and tell him, detail by detail, all of it. He stroked my hair and soothed my pain and cried too. No wonder the Bible says, "Two are better than one . . . If one falls down, his friend can help him up" (Ecclesiastes 4:9-10). He held me, lifted me up that night, and we recognized again all the good reasons that God has put "the solitary in families"!

It was wonderful traveling in Africa together. The trip was exciting. We experienced a military coup, flew in tiny missionary aviation planes, and felt what it was like to live and work in red sub-Sahara sand, bitten by flies and frazzled by heat. We met God's "best" out there on the front lines. We got sick along with the entire population, or so it seemed, and in the midst of it all learned what it was to tell people for the very first time what the folk in "our" world had heard over and over again, for the umpteenth time. The Good News was really good news out there beyond the sound of church and chapel bell.

The missionaries welcomed us as if we were God's gifts to them, and that is exactly how they treated us. To our joy, we began to see how our individual ministries were combining to bring that double blessing we had dreamed about so many years ago. The very struggles we had had in our own experience were mirrored in these people's lives. We talked long and hard about handling ministry and marriage, the challenge of being single, and the struggle to bear the loneliness required to get the job done. Stuart fed their souls with Bible exposition, and we both shared devotional and inspirational encouragement. We listened for hours, played with precious missionary kids, and fell asleep weary with well doing. Finally, we traveled home, more convinced than ever that God had painted us with the colors of our culture and molded us for the ministry together that was now ours.

I realized we had much to share because of those ten preparatory years at Capernwray, and now we had some hard lessons of church life under our belt as well. It was just a question of having the discernment to choose our worldwide opportunities aright.

This didn't mean we only traveled and ministered together, however. There were invitations for both of us apart from the other, and Stuart encouraged me to go for the most strategic of these, helping me to discern which they might be.

Soon I had to sort out the age-old question of women's ministry for myself. I increasingly was being asked to address audiences of both men and women—this time in the context of the local church. I began to read and study in depth and talk the whole thing out with Stuart for the first time. It wasn't the first time we had discussed the issue of what a woman could or could not do in the context of the church, but it was the first time I had been forced to look at all sides and come to my own conclusions about the matter. It took me all of three years to read and listen, discuss and attend classes on the subject before I became really free about taking those opportunities that were often a first for a woman.

"I don't want to be a 'token' woman, Stuart," I said one day.

"Think of it as being a pioneer instead," suggested my husband.

"Promise you'll tell me if you think I can do what I am being asked, or if I'm only being asked because I'm a woman."

"I promise," Stuart assured me.

Having struggled to pull headship and equality together, I finally came to the conclusion it was a bit like believing in predestination and free will. I couldn't reconcile the two, but in faith I accepted both. Sometimes I acted as an Arminian, and other times I was a good Calvinist. So I applied this approach to the "women's issue"—it seemed to work! I came to believe that the man's headship was given him to make sure the woman was equal. Stuart had certainly exercised his headship in this regard. He had insisted on my equal partnership in all matters.

Where ministry was concerned, if a ruling body of a church or mission invited me to exercise the gifts they recognized and confirmed in me, I was delighted to do so—under their headship and in an attitude of humility and submission. I went to serve and not to lord it over anyone. If men in the audience questioned how I was using my gifts (and it has been known to happen), I simply told them I was being submissive to the leadership and the support that had been given me, and referred them "up-stairs." This usually took care of things!

The Lord certainly has brought me a long, long way from the days when Angie and I puzzled over whether we should be a blessing to men or not. Humorously enough, it has been men who have set me free to exercise gifts some other men say I shouldn't have! When men debate "my gift" nowadays, I ask them to be gentle with me and instead of saying "women can or cannot do this or that," to try putting my name in there and say instead, "Jill can or cannot do this or that." Those who know and love me find that difficult to do! Gifts, I have discovered, are not gendered. I undoubt-edly owe the ministry I now exercise worldwide to a hus-band who believes this with all his heart.

I sometimes wonder how many people would have been helped into the kingdom, encouraged by my writing, or challenged into service if my Stuart had not changed his ideas on women's ministry. I suspect not too many. And I think I would have become bored, frustrated, and angry— and not much use to anyone at all. For this freedom, I praise God and thank Stuart, and all the wonderful men in my life who have so consistently and insistently encouraged me to go for the gold with the gifts that I've got and, what's more, have given me opportunities to do so.

Meanwhile back at the ranch, wedding bells were beginning to ring. I never dreamed our children would get married so young, except Pete. Pete we all expected to marry very young. When asked at various meetings to talk about our kids, I used to quip, "We have David who's married, Judy who's married, and Pete whom might very well be married before I get home!" And yet Pete, whom we expected to be married first, was married last, and actually was the oldest of all the kids on his wedding day. This began a new phase for Stuart and me and one that was once again to bring its own rich depths into our own relationship.

As each of our kids chose their partners, we recognized that God was answering a lifetime of prayer for them. We trusted their choices and opened up the family circle to make room for three perfect strangers to take our kids' hands. We discovered the art was to make sure they took hold of our hands, too, so that the family circle wasn't broken.

We had worked hard to help the children look for the right potential qualities in their girlfriends and boyfriends, to be idealistic yet realistic. To search for a Proverbs 31 person in the making, not made! Stuart and I knew it took a life of commitment to marriage to produce sterling character that matches the wonderful model of Christian virtue in this passage.

We helped the children as much as we knew how to look beyond the "What does he look like and what does he do and where does he live or go to school?" to the all-important "What is he like inside?" We encouraged them to ask a far more important question than "Is he a Christian?"—to stretch higher than that and instead inquire what "sort" of a Christian is he? Will he make a good father, will she love her kids, how does he treat you, and how does she treat us? Three weddings later I peruse the scrapbooks and hold the memories close to my heart—savoring the moments and always finding the tears springing easily to my eyes.

For myself, I set about early making friends with my children's choice choices. I took Greg out for a pancake breakfast, shopped with Debbie, took Libby with me to meetings, or made a date for an evening meal just to chat. I tried to give gifts of time, not things for birthdays and Christmas presents, creating an environment where love and mutual respect and understanding could grow. I resolved to say "sorry" often and to keep short accounts over even a hint of a misunderstanding, and pick up the phone to chat with those new young adults in our lives, as well as to our own. I tried to discipline myself to take their side first in a dispute and tried not to decorate their homes, suggest what they should do for their vacations, or comment on their clothes or lifestyle. All of this went against my sinful nature and didn't always happen as it should!

But I determined before God to make *mother-in-law* the best-sounding name in the world´ to Debbie, Greg, and Libby. Above all, I prayed for them fervently and without ceasing and constantly told them so.

Both Stuart and I determined to verbalize our appreciation, too; to thank those precious new couples for loving us and giving us so much of their company, for the fact that they really seemed to want to be around us or to have us be around them. They became our closest, firmest, and most fun friends.

As I finger the wedding poems that I wrote for each occasion, I think so thankfully of each new "unit." I remember standing at the microphone and seeing Debbie's incredibly beautiful, wide blue eyes fastened as if forever on her David's face. I'm sure she didn't hear my poem—and I'm sure Dave, lost in the wonder of his love, didn't hear it either—but it didn't matter. I put my thanks on record anyway, saying to Debbie . . .

> Thank you for lighting up Dave's life
>   with those huge eyes
>   illuminated windows
>   wherein love lies.
>   Communicating brilliantly
>   that empty space
>   incapable of making sense—
>   without the other's face—is filled now!

Dave . . .

> We see you stand
>   and like a strand
> of rope bereft of strength or company to cope
> without the other strand to make the difference,
>   say to thee—
> twine her round thy life
>   for she is yours
> in all her fresh and fragile femininity
>   see to it, son,
>   that you treat her
>   always so with dignity

as we see you do today—
like a piece of Dresden china!

Four children later, Deb is still lighting up Dave's life with those illuminated windows of the soul, and Dave is still reverently caring for his beautiful, fragile piece of Dresden china.

And now it's New Year's Eve two years later. This time an evening wedding in soft candlelight, Elmbrook decked in bright red poinsettias, green trees dressed in a hundred points of light. Judy and Greg face me this time, holding hard to each other's hand . . .

I remember the day you called home, Judy—
   "Mummy—I've met a boy—
    in Wheaton's lounge—
He's just like we ordered!"
   "Like Robert Redford?" I asked.
"He's cuter than Robert Redford," you said!
    Remember?
   Your dad and I prayed for "the boy."
    "Oh God, let him love You
     Let him love Judy
      Let him love us!"
Thank you, Greg, for doing all of those things.
For loving God so surely, so certainly
   and with such joy.
And for loving Stuart and me, too.
   For walking into our lives
    kicking off your shoes
     and wanting to stay.

We thank God for your tall tenderness
　　German Canadian caution
　　　intense integrity
　　your happy, helpful hands
　　　for letting me spell your name wrong
　　　　over and over again!
Thank you for loving Judy like you do—
　　for sailing down the stream of her awareness
　　Into the safe harbor of her heart.
Thank you for tempering her fine-tuned tensions
　　so she's not a knot.
Keep her untied, Greg
　　straighten her out.
Get hold of the frayed edges
　　and keep them securely in place.
May she lie still in your hands
　　while you tease out the tightness—
　　tied in tight against herself
　　　twisted over in
　　　　knots of knottiness,
She's no good to you—or to herself—
　　or to the people that she loves
help her not to be a knot . . .
　　yet, give her room to breathe
　　　and space to grow
　　as she seeks to live
　　her life the shape of the "A"
　　　she desires it to be.
　　　　And
　　may God couple your
　　　coupleness with love's laughter
　　lacing it up with security's strings
　　　marrying it
　　　　to a future that's a home
　　　　　for Himself.

And then much later, in the same church, the same day, the same candlelight and Christmas trees and bright red flowers, but celebrating the uniting of such a different couple. Pete, six feet, six inches, and Lib, all of five feet-two, standing together in sheer exuberance to hear my words for them. Unfortunately, I'd totally lost my voice, so nobody could hear my words for them! So Judy read my "story" for me while I stood by her side . . .

This is a true story. The names have not been changed to protect the innocent! . . . In the beginning there was God. He made a little world in a corner of his big sky and put a lot of little people in it. He stuck them on with a tube of gravity and told them to love each other and be busy.

One day God looked down from heaven and saw a little Libby person running around her eight-year-old world busy being busy! She was the busiest little girl you could imagine. She was busy—growing masses of lovely hair the color of sunshine and making the piano sing. A lot of her time was taken up with making sure her brothers and sisters understood that being number four was just as important as being number one, two, and three. The rest of her energy was spent happily responding to her father's great love for her and building bridges to walk over into the heart of the mother she adored.

God looked down from heaven and saw a little Peter person too. He was eight years of age as well. He was busy not being busy! Well, that's not really true. He was busy watching soccer, reading the Guinness Book of Trivia, *and generally laughing at life. Wherever he went he seemed to have a ball of one sort or another growing out of his hand.*

Years and years went by. The Libby person and the Peter person went away to college, and there they came to really know the Father God who had been watching them from heaven all of this time. Both experienced sadness, struggles, temptations, and failure, and found out the Father doesn't promise a sparrow will not fall, but that a sparrow will not fall without the Father. Standing somewhere in the shadows they found Jesus was the only one who cares and understands; standing somewhere in the shadows they both found him and they knew him by the nail prints on his hands. They both came to love him very, very much.

One day back at church when they were both twenty-two, God put those nail-pierced hands around their hearts and gently blew on a little flicker of love until it sprang up into a firm flame warming their lives—love does that, you know. They wondered how it could be that they had never really "seen" each other before. Perhaps it was because God's clocks keep perfect time and he synchronized their hearts to know the day and hour of his appointment.

The Libby person was still small in frame, a tiny package of dynamite waiting to detonate all that determination into helping and healing. She had such small hands but such a huge grasp of God's truth that sent her out into her world—looking for hurting people and searching for birds with broken wings. Tiny feet, yes, but those little Libby footprints were making large tracks for God as they headed off for heaven in a straight line.

And the Peter person had grown a heart of love that matched his height and strength. God gave him tall thoughts that enabled him to see his world from the heights and dream big dreams that demanded to be realized. He had a strong body but was a gentle man. He had been so easy to raise, easy to praise, and so easy to love. He loved tiny things—like Libby and little children too. Small children knew he loved them and would climb all over him as if he were scaffolding.

Instead of spending his life, the Peter person decided to invest it. So he chose to work with junior high kids because he knew a lot of parents were very bewildered wondering what they had done to deserve a junior high kid happening to them. The Peter person knew that "boys would be boys," but if everyone would only just wait awhile, one day boys would be men. The Libby person shared the Peter person's love for junior highers, and they both thought the very best thing that they could do was to take ninety of them away to camp four days before their wedding!

When Judy had finished and it was time to pray, I took the microphone and whispered my prayer as best I could into the metal head. This part I had to do . . .

Oh God—
  Here we are standing in the
    soft light of candles
      shadows of your
        love
  playing on our children's faces.
Oh Jesus—
  We're glad you are here at our wedding.
  Thank you for loving this Peter person and
    this Libby

person so much
   that it pleased the Lord
to bruise You
   on their behalf.
Oh Holy Spirit—
  Give them, we pray, years of health
    and strength
    to serve you.
Let them never forget to live on the brink of
    eternity
  That looks over the edge of our world
    to the real life ahead
  where people will truly love each other
    without bitterness and anger
    without jealousy that tears lovers apart
  without hatred and hostility and all
    the selfishness
    that makes love limp
  wounded to a bed of pain!
  May their years on earth
  be mingled with eternal blessings
  and may they always know
  that what matters most is
    Jesus!—
    the Name they love, a Friend they count
  as dear as each other,
    the One whose love surpasses
    all other loves
      even their own.
Oh Father God, as you have brought them to
    this hour
  may you go with them around the corner of
  tomorrow into their brand-new day!
We commit them to your loving care,

In Christ's name,
Amen.

Though it was whispered, I know that prayer thundered its way into their hearts. I know because they love and care and light up my life with laughter today.

Stuart "married" each couple, battled with his own emotional joy, and announced with great authority at the end of each ceremony—his strong brown hand clasping theirs together—"Those who God hath joined together, let no man put asunder!"

"Amen, Lord," I whispered, "till death, not divorce, do them part. And may each couple say, as we did—'As for me and my house, we will serve the Lord!'"

18

Two Heads Are Better Than One

Stuart

During the course of a radio interview in which listeners were invited to call in their questions and comments, the subject turned to what is sometimes called the "women's issue." As I tried to answer the questions as honestly as I could, it soon became apparent that my position of encouraging women in ministry was not exactly meeting with the approval of a number of callers.

The interviewer, evidently thinking it was time for him to intervene, said, "Mr. Briscoe, I suspect that you only take this position because of the wife you've got." I was a little surprised at his comment but quickly responded, "It might be more accurate to say that I have got the wife I've got because of the position I took!" I don't remember what happened after that.

There is no doubt that being married to a woman like Jill, who from the day of her conversion had shown a desire and ability to serve the Lord in very effective ways, had necessitated me doing some serious thinking about the place of women in ministry. But it was also true that once I had come to some conclusions on the subject, I had worked hard to support, encourage, and occasionally push Jill in her work for the kingdom.

The formative years of my spiritual life had been spent in Plymouth Brethren assemblies, and in those days there was a strict enforcement of Paul's injunction that "the women should keep silence." Before I met her and shortly after her conversion, Jill had been taken to a Brethren Breaking of Bread service, and in her newfound enthusiasm and ignorance of the Assembly's stand on women keeping silence, had led the assembled company in prayer. She was graciously but firmly corrected and went home duly mortified and chastened. Understandably, she was a little skittish about attending my home assembly on the rare occasions when we visited my parents during our courtship and engagement. She also was less than enthusiastic about wearing the obligatory hat!

My mother, who subscribed wholeheartedly to what she termed "the woman's place," as taught by the Brethren, spoke to Jill about it, and to her credit Jill tried very hard to behave appropriately. But one day she confided in me that she doubted very much that she could ever fit into the Brethren scene, adding somewhat pensively that if the Lord really wanted her there, she would be obedient—but it was clearly going to take a work of grace.

I was not particularly concerned, because by this time my own ministry (even though I was still working in the bank) had taken me into churches of all denominations, parachurch ministries, and activities with people who never went close to churches. But I was beginning to feel a little uneasy about the fact that I had subscribed, without question, to the silent role of women in the church while falling in love with a young woman who didn't seem to be wired up to fill the role.

I had the highest admiration for Jill's enthusiastic and gifted work among the teenagers of Liverpool—in fact, I had never seen a woman close to being as effective as she was. So when we talked about "the issue"—sometimes with a little tension—I suggested that she should continue doing what she was doing outside the church and be silent inside the church. I confess that I was as uneasy about this as I was about a missions system that would send women overseas to do a job that they were not allowed to do at home and then deny them the opportunity to talk about it in male company on their return.

However, the "issue" didn't really surface for quite some time because almost as soon as we were married, Jill became involved with the youth around our home—practically all of them unchurched. When we moved to Capernwray there was much to be done, but the main role of the women was limited to the vast amount of domestic work necessary to run a center populated by hundreds of young people. Jill's interests did not stretch to domesticity outside the home, and she soon busied herself in ministry first to the women of the neighborhood and subsequently the youth. It seemed that as long as she stayed outside a church there was no problem.

But, of course, we then moved to Milwaukee and the pastorate. We became acquainted quite quickly with the expectations that different people had of the "pastor's wife," and Jill became quite perturbed as her role was spelled out for her. I had to intervene on her behalf and assure those who were outlining her job description that they had not hired her and, moreover, if they tried to press her into a traditional mold they would probably expect her to deliver what she couldn't deliver and possibly hinder her in accomplishing the sort of things I knew she could accomplish.

An uneasy situation quickly developed as Jill agreed to teach some of the local women whom she later discovered did not attend the church in which we had arrived to minister. The group began to grow very rapidly, and it was soon necessary for them to move out of private homes into a bank and very quickly from there into a cinema—the one in which we later held our morning services. I was beginning to feel some pressure because on the one hand, my primary concern was naturally the church's ministry, but without looking for it, Jill had discovered a rich vein of responsiveness to her teaching outside the church. Understandably, some of the women in the church were disappointed that Jill was not more involved in their activities, and while they appreciated the obvious blessing in the lives of the women who were being drawn to Christ, a number of them were reluctant to change gears and become involved with the new ministry. So it was necessary for me to wear my husband hat and my pastor hat at the same time.

When Jill asked me what she should do, as her husband I encouraged her to do what I knew was most likely to give her a sense of fulfillment—which was to continue what she was doing. But as her pastor, I reminded her that she should try to build bridges to the women of the church who couldn't handle her unorthodox approach and to remember that the women who were coming to Christ needed to be integrated into the life of a body of believers. The problem with the last part of that objective was that these women all had at least a nominal attachment and allegiance to other churches, even though many of them were testifying to a new experience in Christ.

I was very excited to see the response to Jill's teaching ministry, not only because people were being blessed, but also because Jill's gifts were becoming more evident. She had always shown the abilities and attitudes of an evangelist. But I was concerned that when we got to America she should develop a broader ministry for her own good, and also because I suspected she had much more to offer than she had so far shown. She had a powerful testimony, and she could tell it with great winsomeness and effectiveness, but I knew that if she started giving her testimony she would quickly be on the circuit giving the same talk over and over again. I was also convinced that while testimonies to God's faithfulness in an individual's life glorify God and touch people, they should not become substitutes for the Word of God. The group of women Jill was working with were bright, articulate, challenging, and spiritually hungry, and I was delighted to see the way they were pushing Jill to dig deeper. I pushed too! She was losing none of her evangelistic edge, but she was learning how to make disciples who, in turn, were making other disciples.

In a remarkably short time hundreds of women were attending her weekly class. Many were coming to faith or discovering new vitality in their existing commitment to the Lord Jesus, and quite naturally they, in turn, began to introduce their families to the growing church. Invitations began to come in for Jill to speak in different cities, and the family warmly encouraged her to accept them. She has never found travel easy, and despite appearances to the contrary, she much preferred to stay home, so we had to be careful not to encourage her too enthusiastically.

This new arrangement introduced a new situation—a kind of role-reversal—where Jill went away and I stayed at home with the kids. I thoroughly enjoyed being Mr. Mom, and my three teenagers and I had such fun during Jill's absences. She would call home each night from where she was staying, anxiously inquiring if everybody was all right. At times she confided that while she was happy we were doing fine, she was a little sad to be missing the fun back home and slightly hurt that we seemed to manage okay without her.

On one of Jill's trips Mrs. Pat Zondervan heard her speak and told her husband, and he contacted her, as he had contacted me years earlier, offering her the opportunity to submit a manuscript for publication. It seems strange to relate now—more than twenty-five books later—that she was reluctant to attempt this assignment, but once again we prevailed upon her and *There's a Snake in My Garden* hit the bookstore shelves. It was a little ironic that I, having encouraged her to write the book and helped with the title, should be subjected to much good-natured ribbing by friends and colleagues who guessed the book obviously must be about me! The success of the book paved the way for many more opportunities to address various groups, which were not limited to women.

Now we really had to face the "issue"! Was Paul's statement "I do not permit a woman to teach or to have authority over a man" or "She must be silent" (1 Timothy 2:12) a binding rule for all women at all times in all circumstances, or was it in some way limited?

At that time there were very few books on the subject of women in ministry, so we read what we could and talked to those who would talk about it. One respected pastor said he felt that if the male leadership of a church invited a woman to speak, she could hardly be charged with *usurping* (King James) their authority. This was fine as far as the authority side of the issue went, but it didn't address the issue of women teaching men, assuming, as many people apparently were, that the *teaching* and the *usurping* were two separate prohibitions.

Others pointed out that in the same set of instructions Paul wanted men to raise their hands in prayer and he didn't want the women to wear gold, pearls, and expensive clothes. Since these instructions were regarded as culturally relative, so too were the instructions concerning women, these people claimed. The problem with that position, of course, was that Paul based his argument on the creation order of Adam and Eve and the events of the Fall, both of which could hardly be regarded as purely cultural events. Then there was the perplexing statement about women being saved in childbirth. We were acquainted with a number of possible interpretations of this passage but frankly found some of them more ingenious than convincing.

Paul's clear appeal to the early chapters of Genesis required us to look there for help and guidance. The first chapter clearly showed that there was no difference between man and woman in their status before God. Everything said of the male applied to the female. In fact, both were made in the divine image and received the divine commission. Genesis 2, however, while not specifically stating some kind of hierarchical order, certainly implied it, and Paul apparently saw it there.

The third chapter detailed the Fall. There we read that Eve was deceived and that Adam sinned with his eyes wide open; that the serpent was cursed; that Adam would have a hard life and eventually return to dust; and that Eve, among other things, would now have her man "rule over" her. Opinions differed as to whether this was God describing what fallen males would do to fallen females or whether God was prescribing a subordinate role to the female. In either case, it seemed to me that redemption was designed to roll back the consequences of the Fall, which included male domination of the female. It was also rather obvious that considerable care and attention has been given to making childbirth less traumatic, and thorns, thistles, and sweaty labor less unpleasant, so undoing male domination could possibly fit into the same category.

In other words, I was finding myself in a position of seeing the validity of both arguments—of those who felt that the women's role should be limited because of divine ordinances and those who saw an increasingly broader opportunity for women in ministry. I studied the word *headship,* seeing quite clearly that it can mean both a "source of supply" and a "figure of authority." But I also saw that authority in the church is the authority of a servant, and I recognized that Paul had stated strongly, in marked contrast to orthodox Jewish teaching, that in Christ there is neither "male nor female." Moreover, I recognized that Jesus' treatment of women was radically liberating given the social milieu in which he was operating, and that Paul was by no means as chauvinistic as some people made him out to be when his relations with women in ministry were properly taken into account.

While all this was going on in my mind and in the minds of my staff colleagues who were studying with me, I received a call from an editor at *Moody Monthly* magazine, asking me to write an article on the subject. After some thought I agreed to do it, deciding to address the issue from a very personal point of view. I freely admitted and recognized that opinions vary considerably for a variety of cultural, emotional, theological, and other less noble reasons. But I said that my concern was that the Lord Jesus had made it clear that he was singularly unimpressed with people who bury their talents.

I went on to explain that he did not speak specifically about his view of those who may bury someone else's talents, but I suspected it would not be favorable. As it was obvious to me that men were in control of the affairs of most churches and, accordingly, were in the driver's seat about what women could or could not do, I wondered aloud if male church leaders were in danger of burying women's gifts.

I also assured my readers that this was not an academic question for me because, in addition to my strategic and responsible position as pastor and an elder of a large church which included thousands of women, I was also the husband of one gifted woman and the father of another and, quite frankly, I was afraid that I might bury their gifts.

As I wrote this article I came to the conclusion that if I was going to be wrong on this issue I was going to be wrong on the side of encouraging women to utilize their gifts to the fullest measure, but whenever possible, to do it in such a way that their actions would not be divisive and their ministry would not be hindered. Jill and Judy agreed, and so I found myself in the position of strongly affirming and encouraging many women (not least my own two!) in their ministries.

K K K K K

Shortly thereafter, it occurred to me that it seemed a little odd that on Mother's Day a man should talk to women about being a mother. So I told Jill that I would like her to take the Mother's Day service. She was decidedly nervous about it, but I strongly encouraged her, even stooping to remind her about submission!

The week before Mother's Day I announced to the congregation that at my invitation Jill would be speaking at the Sunday services the following week and that if anyone had any objections they should address them to me. Only a few people objected. We studied the Scriptures on the subject with those who were interested enough to do it, and the historic day dawned.

The response to Jill's honest, open, humorous, and biblical message was tremendous, not only from women who knew her abilities, but also from men who were hearing a woman preacher for the first time. In fact, I saw one man totally attentive to Jill who had sat immobile and impassive through dozens of *my* sermons! This step served to alert the church to Jill's ministry, and, accordingly, she received a great deal of support and encouragement from the Elmbrook congregation as a whole.

Extended tours of ministry to Australia (with Judy) and South Africa (with Beth Severson, a gifted young intern who subsequently became pastor of women's ministries at Elmbrook) soon followed. Invitations to speak on Christian college campuses were extended and accepted, and Jill began to find her schedule very full. This required numerous separations, because sometimes I was away and Jill was at home, and other times she was away and I was at home. But a new scenario also developed—increasingly we were invited to minister together. The first time I remember doing this type of thing away from Milwaukee was in Arizona. We were intrigued by the specific invitation for us both to speak, so we went without any idea of what we were going to do. We had heard of dialogue sermons and had been told of couples who spoke on marriage together—one would speak while the other would stand alongside, listening with rapt attention and a fixed smile (no mean feat when you've heard it a hundred times). We tried both approaches, and they were unmitigated disasters. The obvious problem was that our well-established styles of speaking were so different they didn't blend, and when we tried to make them blend neither of us sounded like anyone we knew. We tried to blend and managed only to be bland!

Partway through the weekend in Arizona I said to Jill, "Let's simply take alternate sessions; you do your thing and I'll do mine." So we did and we discovered that it worked because the contrast of style and approach (mine more didactic, Jill's more dramatic) served to compliment each ministry. Some said I had spoken to their heads, Jill to their hearts; others, that I had instructed them and Jill had involved them. Of course, people inevitably wanted to make comparisons, many of which were not always flattering. We often had to remind those who told us that one of us was better than the other that we were not competing— we were on the same side.

Naturally, when I was preaching on my own I was often introduced as Jill Briscoe's husband, to which I responded that I was the only man in the world who held that distinction, that I felt it was well deserved, and that it didn't bother me at all as long as they didn't introduce me as her father!

░░░░░░

With the changing attitudes toward women in the church, it was predictable that Christian organizations would begin to look for women to sit on their boards. There was probably a degree of tokenism involved, but on the other hand there were obviously women who had a lot to offer in the decision-making processes of ministries that involved women. Because of her numerous books and her speaking, Jill's name was becoming well known, and she was invited to join the board of *Christianity Today,* not least because they had developed a magazine for women.

The invitation came at a particularly embarrassing moment for me, as I had just informed *CT* magazine that after a long-standing subscription I had decided not to renew. On the receipt of a stock questionnaire inquiring why I had chosen not to renew, I had to be honest and say that I rarely had a chance to read the magazine, but now that my wife was on the board, I expected I would be receiving a free copy anyway!

Jill was also invited to serve on the board of World Relief, where her creative ideas were solicited in order to get the message of their ministry out to more people.

Of course, prophets being without honor in their own country, Jill was subjected to good-natured ribbing from the family on her elevation to the directorship of two prestigious organizations handling large amounts of money, particularly in light of her well-known inability to comprehend a checkbook. I, too, was not immune, being asked pointedly by the family if I intended to go to the board meetings with the spouses of the other board members, and, if so, would I go shopping with them while the directors did their work. My masculine pride, I humbly admit, has not bowed to that suggestion.

Increasingly in recent years we have been invited to speak at conferences for missionaries and for pastors and their spouses. Our united ministry has proved far more beneficial in these situations because the male-female relationships in both marriage and ministry are crucially important, and it is certainly beneficial to have a male-female team addressing the issues.

Many, many times I have seen missionaries and pastoral couples coming to share heavy burdens with us, not only, they tell us, because of our teaching, but because in some way we model coupleness and team to them. Few things give us more joy than that. Because women tend to be more open about their problems than men, frequently I have seen pastors' wives or female missionaries first come to talk to Jill, who has then encouraged the pastor or the husband to talk to me. Then together we have shared and prayed and helped to find answers that have saved marriages, preserved ministries, salvaged families, and averted spiritual disasters.

In the midst of all this business we have found time (you can't make time) to relax together, grow together, and encourage each other. The mutual encouragement comes from refusing to be threatened by each other, by being genuinely interested in each other, and by never missing a chance to affirm each other. The mutual growth comes from listening to each other, being willing to learn from each other, and being increasingly honest with each other.

Relaxing together? Well, we tend to do that on the run, but when you consider where we run, we've had some hurried relaxation in some exciting places like the game parks of Kenya, Copacabana Beach in Rio de Janeiro, the spouting geysers of Rotorua, New Zealand, the outback of Australia, the markets of Hong Kong, the emerald fields of Ireland, the highlands of Scotland, the Alps of Switzerland, the cathedrals of Europe, the pyramids of Egypt, the Sea of Galilee and, of course, the lakes of England. We are blessed people!

19

The Big Five-O

Jill

Stuart has always had such a healthy attitude toward aging. He simply ignores it!

"Jill, you were born at the right time, you've been living at the right speed, and so you must be exactly the right age," he said cheerfully as I peered fearfully round the corner of my fiftieth birthday. He added gratuitously, "You'll be dead on time, too."

The day dawned just the same as any other day in history, yet to me it definitely looked a little bit grayer than any that had gone before. The flowers in the yard hadn't quite the luster they'd had last year, I thought, and the bed seemed so much more inviting first thing in the morning than I'd remembered it to be. Was this what the big Five-O was all about? I wondered. Getting gray, fading like a flower, and staying in bed longer and longer till you didn't get up at all? Stuart teased me to no avail. Looking at me seriously he said, "You really are having a tough time with this one, aren't you?" I nodded.

It had been all well and good talking about the seasons of our love and likening the kids' college years to autumn, but suddenly I felt as if autumn had been exceptionally short and winter was well on the way. I definitely wasn't ready for winter.

It seemed to be so much easier for men, I reflected. They grew more distinguished looking the older they became. Never having felt particularly good about my looks, I now began to avoid looking in the mirror at all. How could Stuart still want to look at me? I wondered miserably.

Even the Scriptures seemed to remind me of my dilemma. Paul talked about being fed up with living in his earthly tabernacle. He said he was ready to strike camp and move into the tent pitched and waiting for him in heaven. Well, I could appreciate the imagery but couldn't in all good conscience echo his sentiments. I didn't want to strike camp yet, even though I fully understood—or thought I did—about getting fed up with living in the old tent. I had a few tent pegs missing myself (my back was giving me trouble) and the old tent was beginning to sag a little, but no—I wasn't quite ready for a new address.

I comforted myself with the thought that Stuart hadn't married me for my looks in the first place, so I needn't worry about that. I tried to wear brighter colors to compliment my graying hair and picked vibrant blooms for the house instead of the faded sort. As for the bed, I set the alarm for an early call and began to walk around the lake to meet my husband, who had already run around it at least once.

Stuart really came to my rescue at this point by teasing me into seeing the humorous side of the situation. Whenever I would become intense (most of my waking hours), he would try to help me let off steam by making me laugh. He pointed out that the beautiful little lake we lived by was two miles in circumference and suggested that whenever I was home I should make a habit to walk around it.

"I may not always have the time," I said worriedly. "Will it be okay if I walk halfway round and come back?" I was far too uptight even to realize what I had said.

Stuart, delighted by my poor math, has never let me forget!

"Age leads to wisdom," a friend said, sagely trying to comfort me. "Just think how wise you'll be." I had a mental picture of a Methuselah-like figure sitting cross-legged on a mountain peak as people trailed to the top to seek my advice. No, that wasn't going to happen. Then publishers began requesting a book on aging. I actually had two requests in one week! That did it. How could I be a help to others when I needed help myself?

I began to research the "oldies" in the Bible for my peace of mind. This began to restore my confidence and helped me get a heavenly perspective. I was amazed at how old Moses was (eighty) when God set him off on his life's work. Aaron was eighty-four, and Miriam was even older. Miriam, in fact, was still bashing a mean tambourine in her mid-eighties, dancing around praising the Lord. Anna, a happy octogenarian, smiled at me from the New Testament, not to mention Elizabeth, Zechariah, and Simeon. Yes, there seemed to be plenty of lively old folk around Christ's world when he came.

But then biblical society seemed to view age in a very different light than our society. I had visited Florida and spoken in retirement centers where age looked like so much decorated dust all dressed up with nowhere to go, waiting in wicker basketware—bored and lonely, often bereft of family. Those who had money waited it out in white wicker, with straw hats and white gloves; those without money sat in cheap rattan, with white cloth caps and tennis shoes and no gloves at all.

Fortunately I had some wonderful friends and colleagues well into their seventies and eighties who exuded life and vitality and were determined to die with their boots on. Many of our favorite speakers and preachers were elderly saints, whom Stuart and I would go a long, long way to listen to. So I decided I had to take myself in hand and start to beat the big Five-O before it beat me!

Why couldn't the last third be better than the other two thirds, I lectured myself. *No reason at all,* I answered me. Maybe the energy level wouldn't be quite the same, I acknowledged, but the wisdom to make better judgments concerning the good use of the time left should make up for that. I looked at Stuart for inspiration.

Here he was five years ahead of me, leaving many a younger man in the dust. I had never seen him better, and despite a couple of heart scares, which proved on examination not to be life-threatening, he hadn't missed a step. Yes, God had gifted him with superb physical, emotional, mental, and spiritual strength. But Stuart had also been a good steward of the same, eating wisely, exercising regularly, and being bound and determined to never stop learning more about life. Number 50 looked pretty good to me when I looked at my vibrant husband.

Just as I began to get on my feet, my daughter-in-law Debbie got pregnant! It was all to be part of my big "50 experience"! Without asking my permission, my kids were about to make me a *grandmother.*

In spite of our genuine and utter thrill for the kids (they had been trying for a few years to start their family), I have to admit I had certain definite misgivings. In particular, what might this new status do to Stuart's and my relationship? From now on I wondered if he would see "grandmother" written across my fair forehead every time he looked at me, with the emphasis on the *grand*. Would he begin to treat me like his mother instead of his wife? Would this whole thing kill the romance in our life? How would I feel, I wondered, climbing into bed with *grandpa,* and how would he feel climbing into bed with *grandma?* I was later delighted to discover it felt no different at all. In fact, having our first grandchild gave us plenty of intimate, wonderful times together that drew us both to new depths.

We couldn't imagine how it would be to hold in our arms a new little eternal person that God and our precious children had "made" together! But we tried to imagine it anyway, savoring the anticipation. We even began to add our as-yet-unintroduced grandchild to our daily prayers. We had always used a photo album each morning we were at home to help us to visualize people better as we prayed for them. Now I added the photo of the ultrasound that Debbie had sent me. We read Psalm 139 and marveled at the miracle-in-process inside the safe, warm home that God had built inside our precious daughter-in-law.

I took my calendar off the wall and began to factor in time with my unborn grandchild. This might sound unnecessary, but I knew with the way we signed our lives away years in advance that time had to be put on the calendar or it wouldn't happen.

The day came for Daniel to become part of our family. I was in Holland leading a series of meetings and was fast asleep, but in the middle of the night, as clear as a bell, I woke to my name being called. I didn't need to wonder why. Wide awake in an instant, I began to pray for Debbie and Dave. Four hours later I fell asleep again. It was absolutely no surprise at all to receive the news the very next day that at the exact time I was praying, Daniel was insisting on being born!

I caught a quick flight back to the States, Stuart and I rearranged our lives in a hurry, and soon we were on a plane to the Twin Cities to surprise the family as they brought their baby home. Once booked into a hotel, we persuaded the hospital to tell us the time they would discharge Deb and the baby and hid around the corner of their seminary flat. As we waited breathless with excitement, the kids arrived and we heard Debbie crying, overcome with the magnitude of the occasion. "Oh, what have we done! What a cold, cruel, dark, terrible world we've brought you to, little Daniel," she cried. We could certainly sympathize with her sentiments. He was so tiny and vulnerable, and the night was indeed bitter and dark. But there was plenty of warmth to offer.

What a shock for them when we came around the corner of the corridor. "Oh," sobbed Deb. "You came, you came!" We stood together, arms around each other, cradling that five-pound, fifteen-and-a-half ounce bundle of new hope in the circle of our love, and celebrated the first of a new generation of Briscoes!

He was the most beautiful baby, of course—named after Daniel, a man greatly beloved of the Lord. I bought a T-shirt with the words, "Beware, Grandma with Pictures" emblazoned all over it and set about making sure Daniel David was glad he had a grandma.

Michael came next, a little brother for Daniel to love and play with, and then a bare two years later, twins—Christie and David.

"Are there twins in the family?" inquired a friend.

"There are now," Stuart responded with a grin.

At exactly the same time God was knitting two together inside Debbie, he was knitting one together inside Judy. In fact, the three babies arrived within forty-eight hours of each other. The day our daughter called to tell us the great news that she was pregnant, I admit to a moment of total confusion and speechlessness. How could a daughter be a mother? A child bearing a child seemed somehow to require different adjustments to a son fathering one.

Now Judy and I had another common bond besides our femaleness. I stayed up the night she gave birth. Wrapping myself in a warm blanket, I took my Bible and flask of coffee upstairs to the study and began praying through the Psalms for her. For Judy it would be different than it had been for me, I thought. Greg would be there, for one thing; as knowledgeable about the birth process as his wife, for another. I liked the idea and was sorry Stuart and I had missed that part. These were different days than the days our children had entered the world, that was for sure. Not better—not worse—different!

But the pain would be the same, and the birth would require the same hard work. *It's not called labor for nothing,* I ruminated. My little girl would experience the same unbelievable joy that a child had been born into the world that I had experienced, and she'd know eternal wonder at her small eternal child. I knew she would count his fingers and toes as carefully as I had done and begin wondering who he was like as eagerly as all of us would wonder as we hung over his crib billing and cooing. She would never be quite the same again—how could she be when part of her and Greg was lying in her arms? This little one destined to be, wonder of all wonders, a father himself one day!

Again a quick trip to a hospital. In Chicago this time. There we found ourselves gathering each other in our arms, our body language speaking eloquently our desire to welcome little Andrew Gregory into our hearts. We promised him then a legacy of Christian love and prayer care that is the privileged present of every regenerate family.

Strangely enough, the big Five-O had shrunk to more appropriate dimensions. In fact, the more grandchildren that turned up, the younger I began to feel. I reckoned that once fifty-one came along, the battle would have already been won. Once I had resolved to grow older without growing old, the rest seemed simple!

There were still little hassles that had to be dealt with, of course. My physical activity couldn't keep up with my mental activity. And speaking of mental activity, I began to notice occasional but definite lapses of memory. Stuart assured me they had been around as long as he could remember, and that's probably true. But now I began to notice them. This didn't worry me now, however; I even giggled at the little rhyme I'd heard—

> My glasses come in handy,
> My hearing aid is fine;
> My false teeth are just dandy,
> But I sure do miss my mind!

I realized, though, that the aging process would bring limitations on my mind and my body.

I knew that how I dealt with the resulting frustrations would determine my future usefulness. When my mind would go a hundred miles a minute and my body couldn't keep up with all the ideas and plans, I learned to run the *I would love to do's* through the *what would he love me to do* screen. I asked what was the most strategic, appropriate, and useful thing to accomplish. It was a question of what should I do, not what would I do! But then it had always been so. It was just that now a new sense of urgency hung around my day to alert me to Paul's injunction in 1 Corinthians 7 to redeem the time.

"There's great freedom at this stage of our life, Stuart," I commented one day. The church had just agreed to a restructuring that meant Stuart would retain the position of senior pastor, but would give much of the administration over to colleagues. He himself committed to the pulpit a minimum of twenty-six weeks at Elmbrook. The other twenty-six weeks he was free to be on the road. "We've completed twenty years in the church," I remarked, "and yet in some ways I feel we've just begun!"

It was a great feeling, however, to contemplate the next stage of ministry—and this, we hoped, would at last be together. Well, *almost* together or *sometimes* together. By this time we knew it would not be always together!

As we shuffled through the stacks of letters representing invitations to minister to the church from the four corners of the world, we tried to prioritize the piles. There were many opportunities to be the team we wanted to be, and we took those first. They included pastors-and-wives' conferences across New Zealand, Wycliffe Bible Translators conferences in Indonesia, meetings with Christian leaders in the Baltic states, family conferences in Northern Ireland, summer camps in Europe, and a couples' conference in the good old U.S.A. Down they all went on our calendar.

As we began to implement our new structure, we found a complementary pattern of ministry evolving. "You go for the heart, Jill, while Stu goes for the head," a young minister told us. A psychiatrist listening to both of us speak at a couples conference, commented, "I've never heard such an example of left brain, right brain in my life!" We knew at once which was which, and I took courage from his remark. At least I reflected he hadn't said, "All brain—no brain! Or egghead and blockhead!"

It was fun just traveling together. Now I didn't lose half as many things as I used to. Stuart would gamely retrieve all my various bits and pieces of hand luggage along the way. We would settle into our new quarters—some luxurious, some sparse, some maximum, some minimal comfort—and Stuart would say (as he has just said), "Well, honey, after five days in a different bed every night, this is home for the next four." It wasn't nearly as hard to settle in quickly when there was someone to come home to at night.

Now we could problem-solve together and discover that two heads are indeed better than one at solving them. We could giggle together over the funny things that happened and the funny folk we are—and help each other over the low points (there's usually at least one of those in the course of every conference). What was more, we could model team service and partnership—try to demonstrate how two people of equal worth and gifting in the sight of God could work together, in unity, respecting each other's strengths and allowing the one to be strong where the other was weak. Above all, we could affirm and confirm each other's ministry.

I tried to stop completing all Stuart's sentences for him—and he tried to go my pace and encourage me to make my dreams reality. One year, when one of my books did better than his, he was genuinely thrilled, and when he preached a classic sermon I sent it to publishers, determined that others should benefit, too. We tried not to let others compare us and insisted we were on the same team. Someone has said, "You can achieve anything as long as you don't mind who takes the credit." We found this to be true. "Let each esteem others better than himself," said Paul. We did!

Our adult kids are our best friends and supporters. They visit us, play with us, pray for us, and worry lovingly about us. They scold us when they think we overdo and assure us of their love and concern every time we talk. What greater base of operation could we have? I know none. Isn't this in the end what the blessings of a regenerate family are all about? We think so. Yes, we echo with Joshua: "As for me and my house, we will serve the Lord."

20

Finally

Stuart

In checking this manuscript I noticed that it began on a 747, en route from South Africa. It is appropriate, therefore (the intervening chapters having been scribbled and scratched on various flights and in various airports) that the final words should be written on a flight from New Zealand about to land in San Francisco. It's been a long flight after a busy two weeks' ministry to hundreds of pastors and their spouses. But soon we can both take a break, overnight that is, because tomorrow I go on to Poland while Jill goes home!

Oh well, things don't seem to change much, and we don't particularly want them to—that's why we're planning to go on doing what he's allowed us to do as long as he lets us do it. That means continued commitment to our own wonderful, growing family; continued service to our loving, supportive church family; continued fellowship as opportunities permit with our worldwide family—all the time bearing in mind those we long to bring into the eternal family of the King we serve.

By the way, it's just possible, having read some of the kind of things that Jill has written about me, that you may have concluded she has a perfect husband. Modesty forbids me to allow that erroneous impression to stand. In any case, the truth will come out sooner or later, so I might as well tell you now. Last night, as I filled out Jill's embarkation form at Auckland Airport (I always have to do it because she is traumatized by the sight of a form!), I had to record her birth date—June 29, 1935. Further down the page she had to sign it (she does that herself), and then I put the date—June 29, 1990. *That's odd,* I thought, then realized aloud, "Oh no, Jill, it's your birthday!" Sorry folks, the illusion has been shattered. But there were two extenuating circumstances—as she had forgotten as well, and we were crossing the International Date Line in an easterly direction. Fortunately, we got to live the day twice—unfortunately, it was on a plane!

Our flight stopped briefly in Hawaii to refuel and for us to clear customs. I said to Jill, "Do you realize what a lucky woman you are to have a husband who flies his wife to Hawaii for her birthday?"

"Yes, dear," she said, rolling her eyes heavenward. "I'm a very lucky girl!"

Me too—lucky man, that is!